TURNING GUT PUNCHES INTO PUNCH LINES

TURNING GUT PUNCHES INTO PUNCH LINES

A Comedian's Journey Through Cancer, Divorce and Other Hilarious Stuff

Greg Schwem

Turning Gut Punches into Punch Lines: A Comedian's Journey Through Cancer, Divorce and Other Hilarious Stuff

Author's Website: GregSchwem.com

Softcover ISBN 978-0-9830250-3-0

Published by

Greg Schwem

Front cover image courtesy of Brett Tuttle.

Author photo on back cover by VidAngel Entertainment.®

Produced and printed in the United States of America.

Greg Schwem

Turning Gut Punches into Punch Lines: A Comedian's Journey Through Cancer, Divorce and Other Hilarious Stuff

Greg Schwem has appeared on Comedy Central, VH-1 and starred in his own Drybar Comedy special, *You Can't Quarantine Laughter*. He is the author of two previous Amazon best sellers, *Text Me If You're Breathing* and *The Road to Success Goes Through the Salad Bar*. After reading *Text Me*, sitcom star Ray Romano said "Greg's hilarious take on dealing with parenting in this age of technology made me LOL, ROFL and LMAO."

Since 2011, Greg has written the biweekly *Humor Hotel* column for Tribune Content Agency. His writings have also appeared in publications including *American Way* magazine, *New York Daily News* and *Japan Times*.

Greg is single, a cancer survivor and living in Chicago. Visit Greg online at www.gregschwem.com.

ACKNOWLEDGEMENT

I don't believe I've ever read a book where I haven't glossed over the "acknowledgements" page. So, thank you, the reader, for not glossing over this one; the one where the author thanks all the people without whom the book would NEVER have been possible. C'mon fellow authors, your book would have been possible without your editor; it just would have contained a spelling error or six.

And yet, it took a lot of individuals to help me talk, and laugh, about myself while helping me cope with the most difficult chapters of my life.

Natalie and Amy, I love you, have always loved you and will never give up on our relationships.

Dan, Ann and Randi, thank you for making me realize that "an eye for an eye" is not the way to solve problems; Karen, thank you for the free counseling sessions and Ty, thank you for support while I received them. Also, for sharing your home and your knowledge of Chicago. Julie, Don, Sarah, Patrick, Jill, Adam, Kelly, Sam, Cathy, Dennis and Christine, thank you for showing me that while friends may come and go, family is forever. Ed, Sherry, Shawn, Denise, John S, Logan, Dick, Cara, Bill, Vicky, Mark, Bob, Jay, Kendahl, Allen, Robert, Tom and John B, thank you for being those rare forever friends. Melissa, thanks for putting so much in perspective simply by concluding conversations with, "at the end of the day." Mom and Sally, I'm going to be fine so you can stop worrying.

Brett Tuttle, from one divorced cancer survivor to another, thanks for your inspirational cover design.

I'm not a big fan of self-help books but found contentment and advice in Lori Gottlieb's *Maybe You Should Talk to Someone* (Gottlieb 2019) and John Kim's *Single. On Purpose.* (Kim 2021)

I am DEFINITELY not a fan of Joe Rogan or his *The Joe Rogan Experience* podcast but found episode 2109 with Abigail Shrier extremely enlightening. (Rogan 2024)

A special shout out to the nurses on the oncology floor at Northwestern Palos Community Hospital who laughed at my jokes, handed me tissues when I cried, cheered my early morning walks through the hallways while tethered to an IV, and provided comfort (and some very powerful drugs) when I needed them.

Finally, thank you to Dr. Felipe Gracias, who changed my outlook on life, and what's important in it, with two simple words:

"You're cured."

PREFACE

I've written two books prior to this one. Once I begin the creative process, my first order of business is to set, in my mind, a publication date. How long will it take me to complete the manuscript, format it, proofread it, design the cover art, send query letters to book agents, never hear back from any of those agents, decide to self-publish, keep telling myself those agents will be sorry later, send the finished product to the printer, and make it available for you, the reader to (hopefully) enjoy? For the first two books, that process took six months.

This book took 22 months to complete, which explains why I'm 60 years old in some chapters and 61 in others.

Despite my hopes that I could write another book in half a year, my first two books didn't involve our country's legal system which, if you're trying to describe it in complementary terms, is "measured."

Anyone who has ever experienced divorce knows it is a blizzard of financial disclosure forms, paralegal-generated emails and briefs beginning with 18th-century-sounding prose like, "Now comes the petitioner…"

It's like hiring a town crier to dissolve a marriage. *Oyez, oyez, oyez, be it known on this June day in the year of our Lord two-thousand twenty-four that Greg Schwem is now divorced!*

My bank account is not exactly grateful for the snail's pace of divorce proceedings, but this book would have been far shorter, or non-existent, if I had hired the lawyer who promised to have me divorced in 30 days. Every delay and continuance meant additional fodder for these pages. Some of the names have been changed to protect those who I encountered at random moments and had no idea their conversations with me would ultimately wind up in print.

What was originally supposed to be a series of quick, humorous stories about the divorce process turned into reflections about new chapters in life, new adventures within those chapters, and what it means to be happy. Laughter certainly is part of that definition.

At some point you may stop reading and say, "This book seems so self-serving. Why do I care that this guy drove for Uber or got dumped by online dates? Is he happy or isn't he? And why should I care? I have my own problems."

If that's the case, skip to the last chapter for it will all make sense. But I hope you find laughter, even just for a moment, in these pages. For, as I have always known, but never really experienced until now, the ability to laugh at life's curveballs is what allows us to continue living happy lives.

Greg Schwem September 2024

TABLE OF CONTENTS

Act I: The Reality

Act II: The Reinvention

Act I
THE REALITY

"I dreamed a woman took me to an open grassy field to show me my own grave. And the grave was open and there was a skeleton laying there, my skeleton, and the skeleton had a big smile on its face. I turned to the woman, and I said, 'Does this mean it's possible to die happy? 'And she said, 'Yes it is.' And I said, 'What do I need in order to die happy?' And she said, 'Adventure.' And I said, 'Do you mean like seeing waterfalls and touring the world?' And she said, 'No. People.'"

– ***Steve Martin*** (Neville 2)

A) The Fine Line Between Comedy and Life

When my lawyer told me the end was near, "end" meaning my divorce, I was sitting in an outdoor café in Rome's Piazza di S. Eustachio, nursing a glass of white wine while awaiting an order of rigatoni topped with pork and smothered in tomato sauce.

Around me, happy couples – well, they LOOKED happy – were speaking multiple languages, preventing me, a sole English speaker, from learning their stories. An Italian couple with a son who looked to be about 10 rose to leave. The father, trying to flex his knees, stumbled briefly, grabbing a chair to avoid toppling onto ancient cobblestones. His son squealed in delight and his wife quickly joined in. Soon all three were laughing.

I had just completed a walking food tour of Rome's Campo de Fiori, an open-air market featuring aggressive vendors vying to sell tourists identical bottles of limoncello, olive oil and black truffle dip. Our tour headed toward the Jewish ghetto, once a scene of unspeakable poverty and hardship but now home to pricey restaurants, shops and cafes. Our guide Luca spoke excellent English although his pronunciation of the "Virgin Mary" sounded to me like "Veg-o-Matic." I realized I was not hearing him correctly when he told our group there were literally hundreds of Veg-o-Matic statues throughout Rome.

I surveyed my tour companions. All were duos; two couples celebrating their anniversaries, a mother with a too-bored-looking teenaged son, a mom and her adult son who announced to anybody listening that he was here without his partner, and two other couples in the midst of late spring vacations.

There were smiles and happiness all around, even from the bored son, once he realized his iPhone was incapable of picking up a Roman internet signal. This country, founded in 753 B.C. and home to everybody from Julius Caesar to Christopher Columbus, to Marco Polo to Donatella Versace, might not be such a bad alternative to viewing his friends' Instagram stories.

Six weeks later, my lawyer said THIS time he was serious; the end could happen any day now. Both sides just had to massage a word or two; in other words, one more sentence to fight over, one more paragraph to add and one more hour to be billed for.

At that time, I was in Atlanta, a trip that included concert tickets to see the Rolling Stones, halfway through their "Hackneyed Diamonds" tour and, amazingly, still selling out football stadiums. Never a huge Stones fan, I nonetheless gleefully accepted a relative's offer of an extra ticket because, let's face it, these guys weren't getting any younger. Better to see them now before the next tour starred The Rolling Stone, singular.

Mick Jagger was 80, for God's sake, and would add another year before the tour wrapped. Keith "Even I Can't Believe I'm Still Here" Richards had also achieved octogenarian status. When the concert ended and the three took a collective bow, Ronnie Wood, at 78 the group's "baby," looked the most winded.

What struck me about the show wasn't just that Jagger could still run up and down a catwalk while belting out "Jumpin' Jack Flash" without supplemental oxygen, but how happy he and his bandmates looked, never mind that they'd been playing that song for over 50 years. During that time, they'd endured fatal drug overdoses, divorces, near fatal drug overdoses, physical altercations with one another and verbal sparring in the press. Millionaires many times over they could have called it a career and lived comfortably long before penning "Start Me Up." Yet here they were, swapping solos, ceding the stage to one another, and smiling like three kids who had just formed a garage band. Again, happiness all around.

Then my attention turned to the audience, consisting mostly of men, many leaning on canes for support, and frizzy-gray-haired women sporting beads and bracelets they'd probably worn to multiple Stones shows. And although I was with my cousin, her husband and their kids, I was still solo. No spouse, partner or child to share in the experience. Just like Italy.

Upon returning from Atlanta, I swapped an overnight bag for a larger suitcase, preparing for a work cruise to Scandinavia. I know, "cruise" and "work" should not be used in the same sentence, but I am a comedian, and somebody has to make passengers laugh in between multiple buffet trips. The itinerary featured stops in Finland and Denmark, recently ranked the world's two happiest countries, respectively. What does one pack for a "happiness" tour? A silly hat? A joke book? Nitrous oxide? I packed the usual amount of clothes and, although I was intrigued at the idea of meeting happy Nordics, my travel documents only featured a single name…mine. Whatever happiness I encountered in the world's far north region would be done solo.

Two days later, while exiting the subway at Chicago Avenue and State Street on a perfect summer day, I checked my phone. My inbox included an email from my lawyer with a court order and six words:

"See attached. You are now divorced."

I rounded a corner and sat on the sidewalk, leaning against one of the city's many pizza establishments. Fellow Chicagoans, walking briskly to work, the beach, the bus or wherever, paid no attention to the 61-year-old comedian, his hands resting on his knees and his head down.

Crying.

Wondering if he would ever be happy again.

It had been this way since November 2022 when my wife of 29 years and I decided our marriage had, as court documents would later confirm, suffered an "irretrievable breakdown" and "future attempts at reconciliation would be impracticable and not in the best interests of the family." The court didn't care about the particulars; she was the "petitioner" and I was the "respondent." Nothing more.

Twenty-nine years. When we said, "I do," Kurt Cobain was still alive. OJ Simpson did not have a criminal record. Nobody knew the name "Monica Lewinsky" except Bill Clinton and White House staff who looked the other way when she was on the premises. We'd navigated more than a quarter century together. Now, I was faced with piloting my own ship, not knowing where it would lead or how rough the waters would be.

Imagine awakening from a coma that began in 1993. Inexplicably, you're perfectly alert and healthy, ready to seize the day. You leave the hospital confines and venture onto the street.

A stranger hands you an iPhone. Unsure what it is, or what it's used for, you stare at it as you enter the crosswalk. A speeding car nearly sideswipes you.

The stranger yells, "You really should download a traffic app." Or, if you're in a large city like Chicago, my hometown, the stranger yells, "Get the app, motherfucker!"

An app? What is that? And what is this rectangular thing you're holding that, moments ago, was displaying the correct time but has now gone dark?

That's how I feel as I awaken on Christmas Eve morning 2022, one month after our decision to part ways and with reality setting in. I am alone, freezing and terrified of the speeding cars in my future.

I am not entirely alone. Also, the heat is working. I don't want to give you, the reader, the impression I fled an upper-class suburban existence to live under a viaduct, surrounded by cardboard boxes, shopping carts and despair. I am staying with relatives near Knoxville, Tennessee and will be spending Christmas with them while my wife and two daughters celebrate in the home I still own, 700 miles away. Normally temperatures in the Volunteer State hover in the mid-50s around Christmas time. However, adding to my misery as a soon-to-be-divorced sexagenarian, our nation is currently mired in a winter storm of epic proportions. Southwest Airlines is imploding before holiday travelers' eyes, cancelling upwards of 80 percent of daily flights. Various spokespersons and even Transportation Secretary Pete Buttigieg, a man whom I admire and would admire even more if I could spell his name correctly, are running out of reasons for the meltdown. It will be only a matter of time, I reason, before Secretary Pete appears on FOX News, stares straight at the camera and announces cancellations will continue because "Jasper lost the keys to the garage at Love Field in Dallas and that's where we keep most of the planes. He has been relegated to desk duty while we assess the situation and try to locate a locksmith who is working over the holiday."

FOX News will, in turn, blame the Democratic Party.

Television news reports depicting the carnage show something resembling a luggage fire sale. When one passenger finds his or her bag among the thousands left unattended in baggage claim, other passengers joyously do everything short of forming a flash mob, slightly altering the words to the Mariah Carey Christmas classic and, in unison, singing, "All I Want for Christmas Is My Luggage." Then they return to realizing their Christmas dinners may consist of whatever is left in airport vending machines. Should that occur, Southwest has promised complimentary meal vouchers.

Meanwhile, the entire state of Tennessee is freaking out and that's not an exaggeration. Tennessee is rapidly becoming populated with residents who have relocated from colder climates, know what subzero temperatures feel like and know how to operate shovels and ice scrapers. They abandoned both when choosing

Tennessee because, as they brag to their friends still living in the frozen Tundra, "It *literally* never snows here."

Translation? "It DOES snow here and when it does, we have no idea what the hell to do."

Tennessee streets are deserted, and stores and restaurants are closing as if the Apocalypse is finally upon us. Residents are flocking to NextDoor, the neighborhood information app used by people who really need to take up Pickleball or find something, ANYTHING, to do other than open their laptops, state the obvious and, eventually, pick online fights with fellow users who probably live next door, hence the app's name:

Power went out in my house at 7:32 a.m. Anybody else?

I lost mine at 7:26.

I read that we're going to have rolling blackouts. I'm surprised neither of you knew that!

I'm a retired power company executive and I could have told you years ago that our grid was failing. This was bound to happen.

So why didn't YOU do anything about it?

Yeah, Mr. Wikipedia. If you weren't so selfish, and hadn't kept that information to yourself, maybe I wouldn't have to keep restarting the oven to cook the ham I was planning on making for my relatives who are visiting. Three of them have incurable diseases so this will definitely be their last Christmas. It's a shame assholes like you have already ruined it.

Thanks a lot, Biden!

Wait, power just went back on at my house.

Mine too! Wishing you all a safe and happy holiday.

God Bless You.

Four days later, I found myself in a perfectly ordinary Hyatt hotel on the outskirts of George Bush Intercontinental Airport in Houston. I made it there only because my ticket said "United," not "Southwest." No need to wait on hold for Pete Buttigieg.

Hotels built within two miles of airports are designed for one purpose: Give guests a bed to sleep in, take their money and get them back to the airport as quickly as possible, usually via a shuttle bus driven by a guy with a questionable background. OK, three purposes. Sure, these hotels have restaurants, lame gyms featuring one of everything - one treadmill, one elliptical, one towel – and possibly one pool, but they aren't exactly designed for the leisure traveler. Nobody ever books a seven-night family vacation at the Best Western LaGuardia.

As I exited the restaurant and made my way across the lobby, I noticed another guest standing at the elevator but, instead of waiting for the doors to open, he was facing the opposite direction, staring intently at me. As I got closer, his stare only deepened. Finally, he said, "Greg?"

"Pat?" I replied.

"What are YOU doing here?" we said in unison.

Pat was a fellow Chicago comedian and enjoying a great deal of success. For several years he had been the opening act for Sebastian Maniscalco, an Italian-American comedian regularly filling 15,000-seat arenas. When not opening for Maniscalco, Pat was beginning to headline theaters across the country and had earned every right to do so. We stared at each other briefly, flabbergasted at the timing of our encounter. I assumed he was in town for work, but instead he was visiting a friend in Houston and preferred accommodations near the airport.

"So, what's been going on?" I asked.

"I'm getting divorced," he replied.

"So am I." And then, "We need to go to the bar. Now!"

We headed back across the lobby, sat in a booth, and recounted our stories. Pat had three young children and was dealing with custody issues. His situation, I decided, was more complex than mine.

Eventually the conversation turned to comedy. But the previous topic hung like an elephant in the room.

"Are you talking about it onstage?" Pat asked. "It" meaning divorce.

"I want to, but I just haven't found the proper tone," I said.

I went on to say that, in my opinion, divorce is a tricky subject for a comedian to joke about, particularly a male comedian. Come across as angry at your ex and the audience will almost certainly side with her. There would be a smattering of laughter from divorced guys in the audience but…you get the idea. Don't take cheap shots.

Conversely, lament about your situation during your act and that same audience could quickly grow bored, thinking, "I came here to be entertained and to laugh, not to listen to some guy whine about his personal life. Now please stop telling me you miss your dog."

But, as I reminded Pat, we comedians are always looking for subjects a majority of audience members can relate to. Divorce certainly fits that category.

"Two-thirds of marriages end in divorce," I said. Actually, according to 2022 statistics compiled by Forbes

Magazine, the number is closer to 43 percent for first marriages but let's not argue. (Bieber 2024) No need to give the divorced community one more subject to fight about.

I continued. "I want to talk about divorce but only if I can get people to laugh about it."

Then, I revealed the first joke I had written about this uncomfortable subject. One that IS getting laughs, minus the boos and groans.

"Friends who know I'm getting divorced are checking in on me. They've been asking, 'Greg are you taking care of yourself? How's your physical health?'

I said, 'It's GREAT. I WALK to the liquor store every night.'"

Pat laughed. It was a genuine laugh, not one of those forced, polite laughs comedians emit when they know another comedian is testing material.

Fast forward to the day I received my lawyer's email stating "it" was official. He probably has his eye on a Florida vacation home, one he can now afford thanks to me. I have dabbled in therapy and will most likely resume it.

My wife and I text occasionally but have only spoken once face to face. While it was cordial, it obviously solved nothing. But this book will not dwell on those subjects because that would be whining, and I've already covered my reasons for not doing that. Lives have been disrupted, feelings hurt, questions remain unanswered, and, before it's over, my therapist and my lawyer will be next door neighbors in Florida. In other words, this book is not a "tell all" or a chance to state "my side."

Instead, I am determined to take unfunny subjects, make them funny and make you, the reader, laugh. Divorce, cancer, loss of employment, loss of money; one can laugh at all of them. Just like COVID.

"Wait," you're probably wondering now. "You think a disease that's killed over a million people is FUNNY? What kind of a sick, twisted moron are you?"

It's debatable how sick and twisted I am. After all, I am a professional comedian. And no, COVID is not funny. But think of the situations we found ourselves in thanks to COVID and the two years of lockdown that ensued? The virtual schooling? The online holiday "parties?" The company Zoom calls? How hard did you laugh at the viral video of Texas attorney Rod Ponton, best known not for his judicial skills, but of his resemblance to a white-haired cat? During a virtual court hearing, conducted over Zoom, Ponton couldn't figure out how to turn off a filter designed to make him look like he wanted to lick himself, claw at furniture and then sleep the day away.

"I'm here. I'm not a cat," a flustered Ponton told Judge Roy B. Ferguson. Eventually, Ponton returned to human form although I was thinking a shark filter would have been more appropriate. I mean, he IS an attorney.

Like Ponton, my divorce resulted in numerous unfamiliar situations, best dealt with through humor. Comedians choose our profession because we want audiences to laugh at their stressful lives; to forget about their personal crises for an hour or two. Before I take the stage, be it at 9 in the morning or 11 at night, I say a silent prayer, asking God to help me "make the audience feel better after hearing me than they did before I took the stage." It's not those exact words but I believe He is listening, for I have been blessed with making people laugh, full time, for over 30 years. I primarily perform for corporate audiences, consisting of Fortune 500 companies or professional business associations. Besides jokes, I add a motivational message which is basically, "Even the most traumatic subjects can be funny. You just have to look for the humor."

I've said it during hundreds of performances. I've said it in over a dozen countries. I say it, then I collect a check, then I leave. I've never had to actually *live* those words. Until now.

That is the point of this book; to mine humor from the most unfunny, and possibly unfamiliar, of topics, depending on your life experiences so far. Loss of income, loneliness, a personal health crisis and, most certainly, marriage. When you kiss your mate in a church, a courthouse, beneath an active volcano in New Zealand because you're in your late 20s and you thought it would be fun to have a "destination wedding" or wherever you said, "I do," you have no idea what lies ahead. Yes, you and your partner will share some laughs. But there will be plenty of tears and plenty of "what the hell have I done?" and "what the hell do I do now?" moments. Even if you feel you are happily married, remember the statistics. You could easily find yourself in that 50 percent category, though you may insist otherwise.

"I won't get divorced. I've found my 'soulmate,'" I often hear.

To that, I say, "bullshit." There are nearly 8 billion inhabitants roaming the earth. You have a better chance of winning Powerball than you do of finding that perfect match. You have found a person who, for the moment, shares your recreational interests, your tastes in food, your vacation destination choices. You feel *compatible* with this person, and you do your best to remain compatible until death do you part. But it takes work. Just ask the Stones. There were moments in their show when I noticed the three not only smiling at one another but laughing. I mean, REALLY laughing. They laughed and joked with the enraptured fans about their ages, their voices, or their amazement that they could still remember their own music and lyrics. Maybe humor is what kept them together since 1962, the year of my birth.

So, if you find yourself financially strapped, alone or worse, alone and depressed, look around and find something funny about your situation. If your health suddenly takes a turn for the worse, do the same, even if physically laughing causes you pain.

During my comedy career, corporate titans have occasionally asked me to write them jokes they can open with when they address their employees, customers or shareholders at business events. I always decline because, basically what they are saying is, "You're a comedian; teach me to be funny."

I can't do that. Humor is subjective and personal. No joke, story or experience is universally funny. I can only recount what's worked for me in my darkest moments. I believe laughter will help you find happiness, but it's not a cure-all. It may also take a change of scenery, a therapist or a career pivot. It will take time but, believe me, it will happen. Be patient.

As the Stones like to say, "You can't always get what you want, but if you try some time, you just might find, you get what you need." (The Rolling Stones 1969)

"I am" is reportedly the shortest sentence in the English language. Could it be that "I do" is the longest sentence?

– *Attributed to George Carlin* (BrainyMedia 2024)

B) Sing Along With, But Don't Listen To, the Captain & Tennille

It turns out love could not keep the Captain & Tennille together.

In 1975, one could not turn on a transistor radio without hearing, within approximately 37 seconds, *Love Will Keep Us Together,* a catchy, eventually annoying, ultimately teeth grinding pop ditty from the husband-wife team of Toni Tennille and (Captain) Darryl Dragon. (Captain & Tennille 1975) The 1970s may go down as the decade containing the most chart-topping hits that, if heard enough, caused thoughts of leaping from tall buildings. Don't believe me? Listen to Debby Boone's *You Light Up My Life* or Terry Jacks' *Seasons in the Sun* on repeat and you too will start looking at skyscrapers with no barrier walls.

The pair could not have been more different, leading one to ponder how they ever met and fell in love in the first place? Tennille was vivacious offstage and on; conversely, her husband, permanently clad in a nautical cap normally worn by yacht captains and Florida retirement community residents, hid behind a mountain of synthesizers and rarely spoke, even during the couple's short lived television variety show. *Love Will Keep Us Together* shot to the top of the Billboard charts in June

1975, stayed there for four weeks and ended the year as the number one single. Which meant millions of Americans, while headed to the beach, were singing lines like:

Young and beautiful
Someday your looks will be gone
When the others turn you off
Who'll be turning you on?
I WILL, I WILL, I WILL!

In Tennille's case, no, she won't.

After 39 years of marriage, millions of records sold and years spent touring the world singing about *Muskrat Love,* another single that will eventually have you searching for a ledge 100 stories in the air, the pair split in 2014. Tennille was 74. Her captain was 72 and died five years later. As I write this, Toni Tennille is 83 years old, which blows me away, as I will forever remember her as that gregarious singer with the long bowl cut hair and teeth three sizes too big for her mouth. She reminded me of the soccer mom who, if another mom forgot to bring post-game snacks, probably had three dozen, peanut-free cupcakes in her car, just in case.

The Captain & Tennille were among the more famous of a demographic that is divorcing more than any other: The aging Baby Boomer. I fall into the Baby Boomer category although I was dragged into it kicking and screaming. Boomers were, by most definitions, born between 1946 and 1964. I entered the Earth in 1962 and feel it is unfair that I am lumped into the same generation as humans conceived one year after President Truman decided to drop atomic bombs on Japan and, to this day, refer to the hapless victims as "The Japs." THOSE people are aging; I'm not.

I am also a member of another demographic, one whose numbers doubled between 1990 and 2010, and one that shows no signs of slowing. I am a Gray Divorcee.

Google "Gray Divorce" or "Grey Divorce" and you will eventually become familiar with Susan L. Brown, a sociology professor at Bowling Green State University who has also found time to be the director of the Center for Family and Demographic Research AND co-director of the National Center for Family and Marriage Research. Writing for NBC News in 2021, Brown said her interest in late-in-life divorces was sparked by the split between former Vice President Al Gore and his wife Tipper, married for 40 years. (Brown 2021)

Brown reports that one in four couples getting divorced are over 50, yet the divorce rate overall is declining. Brown attributes this to the fact that Boomers came of age in the 1970s when divorce lost its stigma. People over 50, many of whom are on their second go-round with marriage, feel divorce is the solution to unhappy matrimony, as opposed to their younger counterparts. Brown adds those younger counterparts are less likely to get married in the first place or are getting married later after achieving some sort of independence, be it financial, educational or just vowing not to get hitched until they have completed some life goal…like climbing Machu Picchu by themselves.

I have another theory: Dogs.

Man's best friends may not be the reason for avoiding marriage, but they seem well on their way to replacing children as the species adults love the most and care for until death do they part. Or in the case of dogs, until death does the owner decide to put them down because they just received a veterinary estimate for their pooch's herniated disk. Once, while performing aboard a cruise ship, I casually remarked to the audience that I noticed very few children on board.

The entire showroom erupted in applause.

More about cruise ships in upcoming chapters, but they welcome children. Sort of. Unless you're sailing aboard a ship owned by the Walt Disney company, all cruise ships have a single room known as the "Kids' Club," the "Play Zone," the "Fun House" or another catchy phrase that, in reality means, "a room for parents to dump their children for a few hours so they can enjoy bottomless margaritas." It's an all-encompassing room, full of crayons for preschoolers to create art with, PlayStations for middle schoolers to warp their minds with, couches for teenagers to make out on and probably condoms in case the couch trysts go exceptionally well. The one problem, for parents anyway, is *finding* the Kids Club. Harry Potter had an easier time locating Platform Nine and Three-Quarters. The club is usually tucked away somewhere on the top deck and accessible by only one elevator or staircase. If cruise ship captains could figure out a way to actually tow the Kids' Club behind the vessel, they would do it.

It doesn't take research, degrees and titles to know kids can be the reason couples divorce in the first place or stay unhappily married until the kids have fled the nest.

Which is why millennials, many of whom grew up in miserable family situations and realized they were the reasons, are choosing canines over carpools.

Once, after a show, I struck up a conversation with a young couple from the East Coast and asked if they had children.

"No, we have dogs," the wife replied, with a hair flip and an upturn of her nose.

She said this in a bitchy, yet matter-of-fact tone, as if she and her husband had been given a choice and they had made the correct one. If only it were that easy!

Okay, newlyweds, gather 'round. You have options. You can have a child which, according to Google, will set you back about a quarter of a million dollars by the time it's 18 - half a million if it chooses to play travel soccer - OR you can have a Golden Retriever which eats the same food every day, greets you at the door yet never slams it in anger and will most likely be dead by the time your other option hits puberty.

Hell, if it were that easy, there would be no such thing as "school overcrowding."

Dog shelters emptied during COVID as homebound workers suddenly realized they could not only care for dogs but use them as excuses to work even LESS than they were toiling in this strange virtual environment. If I ever meet Professor Brown, I will ask if COVID played a role in the rising gray divorce statistics. I'm sure it did because the pandemic became an easy excuse for anything unpleasant that happened to those living through it. How many stories that started positively ended with the soul-crushing phrase, "…and then COVID hit?"

"I had just been accepted to medical school…and then COVID hit."

"I got the part on Broadway…and then COVID hit."

"I was ready to start my own business…and then COVID hit."

It would be easy for me to blame COVID, and the ensuing lockdown, for my marriage's downfall. I believed then, and still believe, that my wife and I worked better as a team when we weren't always under the same roof. My job involves intense travel at times and, while some couples can't handle the separation induced by one party's career, other couples embrace, even thrive on it. I placed us in that latter category. Not once in our 29 years of marriage did I ever hear, "You're gone too much; you don't spent enough time with your kids; you love travel more than you love me" or some form thereof.

Which is why, as I drove home from Tennessee in mid-March 2020 after shooting an episode of a travel show I had created, and one which would ultimately fizzle out because …"and then COVID hit," I wondered what nonstop togetherness would bring? I was already in a sour, panicky mode when I pulled into my driveway. While en route, I was afraid to answer my iPhone, or check email, for every message, whether voice or text, was from a client cancelling a speaking engagement and having no idea if it would be rescheduled. Making matters worse was that I drove the entire route, approximately nine hours, in a cold, annoying drizzle. It was the correct weather for the country's mood. At one point, I stopped in a Subway for what I thought would be lunch. While the door was unlocked, all the chairs had been stacked on tables, as if the employees were getting ready to close. A lone worker made me a "to go" sandwich – what other choice was there? – but did so as if she were breaking a law. Maybe she was. COVID had that effect on us. Was it safe to use a public restroom? Kiss our loved ones without masks? Touch a self-service gas pump or a pile of shredded lettuce? In March 2020, who knew?

Truthfully, our issues began long before COVID. And those issues weren't tied to finances, infidelity, pornography, differences in child rearing, or substance abuse, the most common reasons for late in life divorces. I'm sure finances never came into play when another famously gray divorced couple, Bill and Melinda Gates, split after 27 years of marriage. Or maybe they did. Fifty-eight billion dollars, half of Gates' net worth if the couple split everything down the middle, doesn't go as far as it used to. Someone has to feed the family.

We argued a few times early in our marriage about my occasional zeal for marijuana, but it was more of a disagreement than a knockdown, drag out, fight. Nearly 30 years later, I have ceased inhaling but am taking full advantage of legalization in Illinois. Fellow boomers, if nothing else, an Indica gummy is great for sleep. I also have friends who swear by CBD cream to ease nagging joint pain.

Jesus, now I am sounding like an *aging* Boomer. BOMB THOSE JAPS!

No, it became apparent, years before vaccines, masks and Dr. Anthony Fauci - married nearly 40 years by the way - that we had very little in common. That was the long-term problem. I had hoped to tackle that issue once we were empty nesters, a life chapter that seemed about to begin as my oldest had entered the job market with a very marketable degree from a Big Ten university, and her younger sister about to begin her dream of playing volleyball on a full athletic scholarship, at a prestigious East Coast school.

That would leave me plenty of time to teach my wife pickleball, a sport I've gravitated to in the last few years because, once you're over 55, that's the law. I could write an entire chapter, check that, an entire BOOK on pickleball, but that's already been done by hundreds of people who suck at pickleball. So they teach it. Sort of like acting "coaches."

Maybe we'd take a cooking class, spend winter in a warm climate, take cruises together and laugh at the fact that, as a cruise ship comedian, our vacation would not end with a bill but a check. Made out to me!

Instead, I entered a home that included a despondent 22-year-old, searching for jobs that involved logging onto a computer and never meeting, face to face, her co-workers. It became hard to nudge kids of this age, and in this situation, out the door to live on their own. The youngest, meanwhile, had elected to take a "gap year" following her virtual graduation from high school. A weirder event I have never experienced. Here was my daughter, graduating with high honors and being recognized for athletic achievements as well, marinating in her accolades...from the family room couch. Her proud dad, meanwhile, smiled from his recliner, drinking an IPA. The last time I drank at a high school graduation, it was my own.

From that moment on, our lives became two people sharing a bed but nothing else. During lockdown, I hunkered in my home office, demanding silence from the three other occupants, as I was supporting the family doing virtual comedy shows for clients ranging from Microsoft to Merrill Lynch. At an appointed time, dozens of boxes containing distracted, miserable looking faces around the world, most clad in polo shirts bearing their company logos, would flood my computer screen. Their boss would virtually introduce me with a cheerful, "We know it's been hard to find anything to laugh about since March, but we've got a guy today that's going to change that. Take it away, Greg!"

Despite Zoom's immediate popularity, and soaring stock price, the technology was rushed into the world before it was actually perfected. Sort of like letting paying customers board a new roller coaster before testing it with crash dummies. In my case, all participants followed their boss's urgings, and mine, to PLEASE unmute their microphones so I could *hear* laughter. However, if more than 10 people did this, feedback whined through everyone's laptop, desktop, iPhone or tablet, forcing me, the COMEDIAN, to ask everybody to mute themselves. Imagine doing that in a live setting?

Hey everybody it's great to be here. Now shut up while I make you laugh!

By that time, most Zoom participants had already clicked the 'mute' command anyway, turning off their cameras as well so they could help their kids with their virtual schoolwork, run to the refrigerator for a yogurt or leave their homes entirely. I was left performing to silent black boxes containing initials.

When I exited the office after one of these outrageous and humiliating performances, my wife feigned sympathy. And probably interest.

"How did it go?" she'd ask.

"I'm not sure," I said. "I got three 'laugh out loud' emojis in the chat box.

Not exactly something worth putting on one's LinkedIn profile.

When lockdown eased, and in-person events returned, I was only too happy to spend as much time on the road as possible. My wife, meanwhile, had taken a job at an upscale hotel, one which she seemed to enjoy despite having to shut off an alarm five days a week, something she hadn't done in 25 years. My youngest returned to college and my oldest found a job in human resources at a nationwide discount grocery chain. When friends asked about her job, I made sure to say she worked for the name of the chain, followed by "CORPORATE," lest they think I dropped 80 grand on a Big Ten university degree so my daughter could be the head checkout clerk.

Sadly, life didn't return to normal because after COVID, there was no such thing. I ultimately found myself back in Tennessee one crisp fall weekend. College football-crazed Knoxville was in a tizzy because the University of Tennessee had just knocked off number one ranked Alabama. Meanwhile, my relatives told me about a honky-tonk in Louisville, Tennessee that was hosting live musicians that same night. The owner was pleading with mailing list subscribers to PLEASE come out and support the band.

"Let's go," I said.

Off we went, traversing dirt roads with zero streetlights, and waiting for deer, coyotes or grizzly bears to leap into our car's path. Eventually we came upon The Station, best described as "a barn with a bar" although the owners encouraged BYOB. The Station had no website; only a Facebook page touting its wooden interior, intimate seating and outstanding music, provided by any band that could actually FIND the venue. Shortly after 8 p.m. a four-man country band appeared. They ranged in age from a drummer in his mid 20s to a keyboardist who could give the Rolling Stones a run for their money. Not necessarily in talent but certainly in age. The quartet gazed at the third-full venue and realized little if no money would be made that night.

Still, they played their guts out, telling stories, swapping solos, and smiling the entire time. Just like the Stones.

That night I saw four guys doing exactly what they wanted to do in life. They were genuinely happy, even if unlike the Stones, they were financially challenged. It was then I realized that no amount of therapy, cooking classes or trips to exotic or unpronounceable destinations could rekindle the spark I once felt with my wife. I had discovered other reasons for my decision, and I'm sure she did some discovering of her own about me but, as I mentioned previously, this book is not a tell all. What I can tell you is that I hadn't been happy for a long time and divorce appeared to be the only option.

I will be happy.

I will. I will. I will.

"Laugh loudly, laugh often and most important, laugh at yourself."

– Chelsea Handler (Handler 2011, IX)

C) You're Getting Divorced? I'm Sorry . . . or Congratulations!

So what is it like going through a divorce at 60, you ask? It's confusing, frightening and ultimately hilarious. Let me briefly explain.

It's moving out of a 4,400 square foot house in the suburbs. It's realizing you should have begun purging contents from that house 20 years ago, because now you need a costly dumpster to haul useless shit away. It's neighbors watching the shit eviction and wondering if you and your wife had a hoarding problem. It's those same neighbors, upon seeing a FOR SALE sign in your lawn, asking if you're downsizing. Or retiring. Or both. It's those same neighbors asking where you are moving to. It's replying, "Well, I'm moving to the city." It's the look on your neighbors' faces when they realize what you just revealed.

It's moving into a 700-square foot city condo because you wanted a "minimalist" existence. It's discovering you actually have 720 feet of living space if you stack the majority of non-perishable food items on top of your refrigerator. It's shredding your Costco membership card upon comprehending you no longer have the storage space for ANYTHING Costco sells. Now finish that gallon plastic tub of peanut butter-filled pretzels and find something equally delicious, and teenier, to munch on. On second thought, keep the plastic tub. It definitely has storage capabilities.

It's choosing a neighborhood in a city that touts 178 of them. It's listening to city residents describe every neighborhood as "full of young people." It's realizing even a neighborhood known as "Old Town" fits that category. It's finally settling in the Wrigleyville neighborhood, walking down a street at two in the afternoon and encountering a fellow resident in a T-shirt emblazoned with Greek letters, an exploding keg and the year 2023. It's that person smiling at you and saying "Good morning!" It's staring at another resident who looks, at most, ten years older than you, leaning on a cane for support and lumbering toward a city bus stop. It's wondering if city living is indeed right for you. It's joining a city health club to ensure you will never become that cane-addled person. It's noticing every member in that club except you knows the words to whatever hip-hop song is blaring over the speakers. It's watching these people, in between squats, grunts, thrusts and truck tire flips, singing Lizzo's *It's About Damn Time* featuring the line "It's bad bitch o'clock; it's thick thirty." (Lizzo 2022) It's incorrectly hearing those lyrics and thinking Lizzo is actually singing "It's DICK thirty." It's looking at your Apple watch and trying to decide if dick thirty happens in morning or evening?

It's getting dressed, looking at yourself in the mirror and realizing there is nobody to tell you if that shirt goes with those pants. It's buying clothes and having to decide on your own if they make your ass look flabby. It's getting a strange look from the Nordstrom's sales rep when you ask him that very question. It's heading to the health club every day, vowing to work on your flabby ass.

It's washing clothes in your building's community laundry room and being thankful you don't have to schlep your dirty underwear to a laundromat that only accepts tokens. It's pulling up to your building, parking your car in a tow zone while you unload groceries and run them up to your unit, and forgetting you left your car unattended with the hazard lights flashing. It's realizing at 5:30 the next morning that yes, you really did that. It's your doorman telling you the car has been towed to a city pound. It's riding your bike to that pound and paying for some guy to jumpstart your dead vehicle after first breaking into it. It's marveling at how easy and fast it is to break into a car using tools one can buy for 15 bucks on Amazon. It's wondering if your car will eventually get stolen now that you've seen how vulnerable it is. It's pondering if you should even own a car?

It's finally understanding why UberEats and Instacart are so popular.

It's "I forgot I left my car running. Do I have Alzheimer's? Do I have early onset dementia? Who will take care of me if I receive either diagnosis?" It's googling "least painful suicide methods." It's looking down from your 14th story balcony and wondering how quickly you'd hit the ground. Not that it matters, but it's estimated World Trade Center jumpers were only in the air for 10 seconds. It's quickly extinguishing those thoughts and thinking "this should be the BEGINNING of my life, not the end."

It's "why is the bus late? Why am I standing on this L platform freezing my ass off? Maybe I should Uber. Shit,

20 bucks for an Uber to take me three miles? I'll take the L. Shit, I need warmer gloves. I should have driven. Wait, I no longer own a car."

It's friends responding to your divorce with "I'm sorry or congratulations!" It's detecting a hint of envy and admiration in some of their voices. It's divorced people saying "It sucks but you'll get through it and you'll feel better when it's over." It's never hearing from those suburban friends you hung out with for 29 years and wondering why? It's a divorced podcast host telling you, off air, that you're going to have to make all new friends because "your old friends knew you as a couple." It's searching "Chicago" from your Facebook friends list and thinking maybe it's time to reconnect with whomever popped up even though you haven't connected with these people for a decade and there's a reason for that.

It's learning "no contact" is not only a phrase but a movement.

It's "you're still funny, you still have hair, you're still marketable and you still have your health." It's feeling flu-like on a 90-degree September day. It's taking a bus to a primary care clinic you had to google because you don't know where to go when you're sick. It's "you have bronchitis." It's a trip to the emergency room where the diagnosis becomes "you have pneumonia. Also, a spot on your lung. And your adrenal gland." It's numerous prods, pokes and scans that reveal nothing serious but "you should probably be rechecked every six months." It's getting a cancer diagnosis before you've had a chance to schedule the pneumonia follow up appointments. It's realizing your ex-wife has awesome health insurance. It's learning COBRA is more than a venomous snake.

It's wondering if you are ever going to have sex again. It's trying to imagine sex with anybody other than your partner of 29 years. It's slipping a Viagra in your pants pocket whenever you go out for the evening "just in case." It's neglecting to remember it's still there when you return and, when you do, those pants are in the washing machine. It's wondering again if you have Alzheimer's. Wait, didn't I just type that sentence? I can't remember.

It's doing stupid shit like taking the subway at 4:30 a.m.; hiking alone in Alaska despite the threat of bears; lifting objects you know will cause excruciating, lingering pain somewhere; neglecting sunscreen; investing too much money in crypto; walking when you really should be calling an Uber; cycling when you really should be walking. You do this shit because, if you die, right before your lights go out eternally you can say "All in all, no regrets."

It's vowing to do stuff you really should have checked off in your twenties, like learning Spanish, taking a bartending class, backpacking through Europe or tripping on mushrooms, which definitely falls into the "stupid shit" category. It's calling a friend who has tripped on mushrooms and saying you're curious but only if the mushrooms will help you sleep.

It's wondering if that selfie you took after a few margaritas in Cozumel would make a good dating profile picture. It's the ego boost you only feel when Bumble says you've been "super swiped." It's scrolling through potential matches, coming across a woman who looks vaguely familiar and realizing she was your next-door neighbor in your previous life. Yes Michelle, I read your profile but it felt weird to super swipe you.

It's accepting that everyone makes bad decisions in life. They may leave you with less money, fewer friends or poorer health, the latter if you put off that colonoscopy, breast exam, eye doctor visit or annual physical. But when it comes down to it, the only bad decision you can make in life is…

"I think I can beat this approaching train."

"The best stories in the world to me are the ones that elicit a real emotion but have humor."

– *Jim Carrey* (Carrey 2008)

D) Today I Will be the World's Least Interesting Person

Two months after hiring a divorce attorney, over Zoom naturally, I hit the road harder than I had ever hit it in my life. Since taking the comedic plunge full time, I have performed in 48 of 50 states and dream of doing so in all 50 (Hey Vermont and Wyoming, if you're reading this, I'll give you my special "bucket list" rate) and over a dozen foreign countries. While some entertainers loathe the cancelled flights, lost luggage, passengers who fart while asleep – or in some cases, fully awake - and everything else that comes with travel, I find it invigorating. And therapeutic.

At this point I had not opted to write a book, but just to journal what was occurring not only in my line of vision but also inside my head. David Sedaris, one of my favorite humor writers, appears to do this daily; a cavalcade of his entries usually become best sellers. Maybe I'd end up with something similar.

Many of these initial observations occurred while performing aboard cruise ships, venues that consist of plenty of idle time for comedians, along with incredible people watching. Cruise ships, incidentally, are unique venues for entertainers be they comedians, singers, magicians or acts who bill themselves as all three, meaning they don't have the material to sustain a singular credential for a 45-minute performance.

Unlike some of my comedy cohorts, who spend upwards of 40 weeks at sea and now are incapable of writing jokes about any subject other than buffets and lifeboat drills, I've cruised sparingly. I first experienced cruise life in 1989 when I made the decision to become a full-time comedian and was still living in South Florida. Cruise agents LOVE Florida-based acts as many ships depart from the ports of Miami and Port Everglades. No need to pay airfare for a Florida-based act.

A cruise agent liked my VHS audition tape – yes, I've been at this a long time - and offered me two weeks aboard the Norwegian Skyward, a ship that weirdly, embarked from San Juan, Puerto Rico, necessitating a flight. Norwegian Cruise Lines offered me five times the money I was making toiling as a comedy club emcee, so I jumped at the chance. Three weeks later, arriving in San Juan for the first time, I found myself wandering a never-ending maze of corridors and below sea level passageways, searching for somebody called the "Crew Purser." This person's job was to hand me a cabin key and a bunch of contracts to sign, basically stating I wouldn't keep any fruits, vegetables or drugs in my cabin. I was officially a "ship act."

Cruise entertainers don't perform every night, leaving us lots of free time to wander the ship and, if we choose, converse with passengers. This can begin as early as the first evening, when passengers flock to the ship's main theatre for the "Welcome Aboard" show, where the ship's cruise director blathers on for 15 minutes about the FUN that awaits every paying guest and repeatedly uses the phrase "I want to thank each and every one of you..."

I hate that phrase more than "If I can be perfectly honest with you…"

Over the years I've become friends and Instagram connections with multiple cruise directors, but their personalities rarely change. The late David Foster Wallace spent a week aboard a cruise ship recounting his experience in a hilarious essay, *A Supposedly Fun Thing I'll Never Do Again.* His description of the ship's male cruise director had me in stitches:

"It always looks like he's constantly posing for a photograph nobody is taking." (Wallace 1998, 339)

I spied a couple leaning against the back wall, a popular destination with cruise passengers who can subtly sneak out if they don't like what's happening onstage. Today, passengers are bolder; I'd be lying if I said I never saw audience members in the front row decide they'd had enough of me and my attempts at humor.

Sidling up to them, I learned they had journeyed across the country from Seattle for their time aboard the Skyward. I asked if they had ever cruised before and what they planned to do for the next week.

The husband chimed in. "Well, we're on our honeymoon so we're definitely gonna FUCK!"

I wonder how that marriage turned out?

My wife was an avid cruiser, although not necessarily for the reason I just mentioned. Before kids, we enjoyed a few cruises full of gluttonous feasts and bottomless daiquiris. Incidentally, one of those cruises occurred when, unbeknownst to us both, she was pregnant with our first child. Nine months later, our daughter was born perfectly normal, void of gills, clubbed feet, two brain stems or other defects that medical studies say will occur if Mom-to-be wolfs down a few tequila shots. Pregnant women, remember that when your body feels like a truck ran over it and your mood responds accordingly. BOTTOMS UP!

When we became parents, we brought our daughter aboard because it was a free family vacation, albeit a difficult one with a baby. Passengers and cruise staff would watch in horror and amazement as my wife and I lumbered up the gangway carrying a folding stroller, a folding bassinet and a folding diaper bag containing dozens of neatly folder diapers. They'd ask how many months we planned to be aboard.

"One week," we would respond.

When COVID hit and corporate work (my primary source of income) dried up, I reentered the industry just for a chance to perform for live audiences. The cruise ship industry was also on life support and, by some media accounts, was the reason COVID hadn't been eradicated. Never mind that 60,000 sports fans had returned to watching live events in stadiums, sitting shoulder to shoulder and coughing on one another. Desperate to stay afloat (no pun intended) ships re-entered the world's oceans at 50 percent capacity, featuring cruise diehards who were more than happy to sail while wearing masks they would only remove to scarf down copious amounts of buffet shrimp.

Not only was the cruise market a chance for me to return to a real stage, performing for real people instead of Zoom boxes, but as I previously mentioned, I thought it might serve as a fascinating, and profitable form of retirement for my wife and myself. I imagined us sailing to far flung locales. We'd walk with penguins in Antarctica or crash weddings beneath waterfalls in South American rainforests. Plus, we would travel lighter. No more folding diapers.

I performed aboard five different cruise ships in winter and spring 2023, visiting 15 countries in the process. I also did a steady stream of corporate dates everywhere from Washington DC to Orlando, to Denver. Throughout this span, I vowed to strike up conversations with whomever was willing to chat. When not talking, I would be the world's best listener, eavesdropping when possible and gleaning whatever information I could from those around me. In other words, I would be the least interesting person in the room, never mind that as a comedian, my occupation and my stories are almost always more interesting than yours.

What follows is a hodge podge of random thoughts and observations that might give you, the reader, some insight into the thought process of someone realizing he has entered his biggest ever life change. Or maybe you'll just get a few laughs. I'm fine with either.

January 15, 2023 – Chicago, IL. Today I digested a commercial for a heart medication that warned of numerous side effects, one of which was "changes in dreams."

"How would one know?" I thought. One of the great qualities about dreams is their scripts are remarkably different once one drifts off to sleep. Well, unless you count the recurring dream I have where I'm about to take a college final for a course I didn't study for because I didn't even know I was supposed to be taking it and therefore never attended. I've talked to a lot of people who have dreamed something similar. And not all of them were fraternity brothers.

So, I'm not sure if my divorce is messing with my dreams but oh, how I would long for a night of uninterrupted sleep. Last night I dreamed I was the narrator in a children's Christmas play. I was awarded the role mere minutes before opening night but was told there would be a script on downstage monitors and I just had to read the words as they appeared. "Simple enough," I thought.

There I was, surrounded by first graders adorned in red and green sweaters, some wearing reindeer antlers or slip-on, pointed "Elf-like" ears, as we waited for the curtain to rise. When it did, the stage lights malfunctioned and we stood in darkness causing some of the "elves" to begin calling out for their parents. Suddenly the lights went on but there was no script on the monitors and an entire audience of moms and dads, their iPhones aimed at me, waited impatiently. Not knowing what to do, I feigned a panic attack and fell to the ground.

Then I vomited bugs.

I may spend tonight at a 24-hour diner.

January 18, 2023 – Amelia Island, FL. Since realizing my marital status would soon revert to "single," I find myself staring at couples in airports and other public places. I look at their demeanor; the way she tosses her hair when she's with him and the way he pulls her closer via an arm around her shoulder or a hand in hers. I wonder if they are married or contemplating marriage?

Then I imagine them 25 to 30 years from now, dividing their furniture and their finances when at one point, one turns to the other and says "Remember when we saw that guy in the airport staring at us years ago? He seemed like he was trying to tell us something. I wonder what it was?"

January 21, 2023 – Chicago, IL. Even though I am still married, I have decided to officially remove my wedding ring. For the past 29 years the only time I have done so was prior to having an MRI. Come to think of it, divorce and an MRI are very similar in that both occasionally make you feel like you can't breathe and want to flee your surroundings, even if you aren't fully clothed.

January 24, 2023 – Cozumel, Mexico. I am sitting in a hot airport terminal awaiting a flight that will take me to Miami where I will connect to San Jose, Costa Rica. These are the kinds of itineraries one experiences when becoming a cruise ship employee or, in my case a "guest entertainer." We board ships in the middle of cruises, leave before the cruise terminates and have hellish travel nightmares that would put your "I was delayed in Milwaukee for three hours due to a snowstorm" story to shame.

"Remember the time we had to overnight in Ushuaia and were stuck there until they could get us a flight to the Falkland Islands?" the ship's bass player will say to the drummer.

"Yeah, that was rough. But sorta fun too."

Hell, I've seen airline gate agents nearly get physically assaulted because a businessman missed his flight to Fort Wayne, Indiana.

January 24, 2023 – Puntarena, Costa Rica. I think Spanish speaking people are gaining ground in their determination to make their language the world's official dialect. While in Amelia Island I stopped a maid pushing her cart around 9:30 a.m. and informed her that, while I would not be needing service today, I would be needing two towels.

No hable Ingles, she replied, before whipping out an iPhone, opening Google Translate and motioning me to type out my request. I always marvel that anyone, regardless of annual income or status in life, still can scrape money together to own an iPhone and the service plan that accompanies it. I've seen homeless men with iPhones begging for money, prompting me to ask why they don't just download a list of job openings, particularly in the tech sector, since they have telecommunications experience. I know this sounds harsh, but haven't you wondered the same thing?

I typed "Please give me two towels," mistyping every word as is my want when I type anything on a cell phone. I sometimes wonder if some mistyped, and therefore misinterpreted texts, contributed to my marriage's demise. Like the one I typed from a Vegas hotel room:

"I woke up and had no idea what time it was. Why did this hotel remove all the bedside cocks?"

It's times like these when I decide it's high time I learn Spanish. Instead of being angry that the English language is becoming second tier in some countries (and some U.S.

states), why not add a few remnants of a new language to my vocabulary? Saying "double my vocabulary" seems a bit cocky at this point considering my Spanish consists of words like "cerveza," "banos," and now, my first phrase: *Por favor, dame dos toallas.*

"What better time than the present?" I remember thinking when my divorce was imminent and I began spending unordinary amounts of time alone. The last time I had a similar moment of inspiration was a month into the pandemic when reality set in for the entire world that this new definition of "indoor living" wasn't going anywhere and we had already burned through most of Netflix.

"Take up a hobby" screamed the internet, prompting within weeks, accounts of isolation that morphed into success stories. Suddenly everyone was redecorating their basement with home improvement skills they acquired on YouTube. Others mastered French cooking or finished their screenplays and sold them to eager studios. Sarah Cooper, a former tech employee, humor writer and sometimes comedian, posted viral videos of her lip-syncing some of Donald Trump's more outrageous statements. She made a fortune.

I vowed to continue my guitar lessons, after a 47-year hiatus. I could hear my wife and daughters rolling their eyes in the next room as I struggled to relearn chords with the help of the internet and guitar playing apps. My experiment lasted three days before I gave up. But I was able to strum the Eagles' *Peaceful Easy Feeling* with confidence.

I fear the same thing may happen if I purchase an online "Learn Spanish Fast" program. I have already investigated Babble, allegedly the most popular language program, although the title makes me wonder how this could be so. "Babble" is what I'm doing now when speaking Spanish; not what I strive to do. Is the second most popular language program "Jibberish?"

While I can afford the $80 annual fee, I hesitate to spend the money for something I may not complete, although that thought never entered my mind when I was typing my credit card number on the eHarmony dating site. (More about that later). Maybe I can hook up with a Spanish speaking lady and I won't have to pay for lessons.

But my vocabulary needs to improve…and quickly. I am writing this in a public park in Puntarena, Costa Rica. I have just tossed a banana peel on the ground, curious about whether pigeons like bananas. They don't.

I retrieve the banana peel and notice a family of five behind me witnessing the entire encounter. Two of them try conversing with me in Spanish and I have no idea what they are saying. They could be asking if I have a penchant for birds? Or fruit? Maybe they feel I am defacing their country by littering. Or maybe they are just making fun of me, knowing I don't speak the language and can't respond with a witty retort.

Whatever. I want to know. Babble, you will soon get your money.

January 26, 2023 – Somewhere between Puntarena, Costa Rica and Panama City, Fuerte Amador, Balboa. Seeing 26 on the calendar always leads to me doing a simple math equation in my head because my birthday is September 26. So, I can quickly deduce that I celebrated my birthday four months ago and will add another milestone in eight months.

Today all I could think was "It's been four months since I've had sex."

My mind raced back to September 2022 when my wife and I celebrated my 60th milestone via a trip to North Carolina to watch my daughter play volleyball. We spent an additional night in Durham, strolling the hallowed campus of Duke University, having a relaxing lunch in an outdoor coffee shop and yes, making love that evening.

Today, save for saying "Sure, no problem" when a woman approached and asked if she could take two of the four sets of silverware piled on the table where I was answering emails on my laptop, I have spoken to no one.

On a cruise ship containing more than 2500 people, I have had no verbal conversations.

Try going an entire day without talking to anyone except your pets or yourself. It's not difficult but it is mighty depressing when you pull the covers up to your head that night and realize what you've accomplished. Luckily, it's only 5 p.m – there's still time.

Twitter was ablaze at reminders that this day also marked the 37th anniversary of the 1985 Chicago Bears' Superbowl victory. That may have been the only year I wanted to be in Chicago in January. Instead, I remember watching it at a fellow reporter's home in West Palm Beach, Florida where I was working. But it wasn't the same. Chicago friends I'd left behind were calling in the run up to the game saying how bonkers the city was. Chicago may have shitty sports teams but we were blessed to have, in my opinion, the two greatest sports teams of all time, that being the '85 Bears and the Michael

Jordan-led Bulls. Jordan, however, graced our presence more than once a week, which is why the Bears team was so special. And, unlike Jordan, an icon surrounded by an ordinary supporting cast, the Bears had a boatload of players who became marquee stars based solely on their personalities. Start with William "Refrigerator" Perry, add out-of-control quarterback Jim McMahon and, for good measure, include one of the game's greatest running backs, Walter Payton and you had a marketing orgasm on your hands. Hell, even the KICKER, Kevin Butler, had his own radio show.

Sadly, it pains Bears fans to realize what has happened to their rock star heroes. Payton died of a rare liver disease just 13 years removed from raising the Super Bowl trophy, McMahon's brains are so scrambled that he may not even remember winning the championship and defensive mainstay Steve McMichael's body succumbed to the ravages of Lou Gehrig's disease although, as of this writing, he is still with us. Photos of former Bears paying McMichael visits pop up on social media every now and then.

I would love to be included in that group. Just to have someone to talk to.

January 27, 2023 Panama City, Fuerte Amador, Balboa. Just visited cruisemapper.com, which gives the history and current location of every cruise ship in operation. Included with each ship description is an "accidents" tab. I discovered that in 2017, a man murdered his wife while on board the Emerald Princess, where I am currently performing. The crime occurred after she asked him for a divorce.

February 7 – San Jose, Costa Rica. – I am laying poolside at the Holiday Inn Express in San Jose, a stone's throw from the San Jose airport. Which means a lengthy nap is out of the question. Still, I was able to doze for about 20 minutes in between landings. I woke up to hear a girl lounging next to me say to her traveling companion "He murdered her, right?"

Then she began to repeatedly talk about "her ex," leading me to wonder if somehow this story should have been told in reverse.

The hotel is where Princess Cruise employees sleep the night before a van driver picks them up the next morning and drives them to Puntarena, two hours away. Surely there must be a hotel closer but who was I to ask? I was grateful that upon arrival, the front desk clerk told me in excellent English that the ship was covering all of my meals and I had multiple options to choose from. Breakfast, she explained, would be courtesy of the hotel buffet but I could eat lunch or dinner at one of two restaurants within walking distance of the hotel. Those consisted of Denny's and Pirata's, a bar and grill in an empty casino adjacent to the Denny's. I chose the latter.

The idea of traveling to another country and eating in a U.S-based chain restaurant, particularly one that serves something called the MOONS OVER MY HAMMY, seemed sacrilege. My ex and I differed on that. When I chose the restaurant, it was usually something I found on Yelp and located at the end of a dark alley. She opted for The Cheesecake Factory or P.F. Changs, both of which can be found in malls and airports nationwide. The Cheesecake Factory is most known not for the cheesecake, but for the menu which is longer and more tedious to read than this chapter. P.F. Chang's is known for giving me diarrhea.

February 8, 2023 – Puntarenas, Costa Rica. The van arrived at 7 am. By 7:10 myself and two other employees – Ryan, a piano player from Las Vegas and Sira, a front desk staff attendant from Peru, were headed to the port where the Emerald Princess had docked.

By 7:15 a.m. my bladder was not cooperating.

One of the pitfalls of being male, and living past 60, is that a prostate, urethra or any other body part involved in the simple act of urination, could malfunction at any time. I try to shun fluids before lengthy travel trips but I could easily swallow a bucket of sand, kitty litter or any substance that absorbs liquids and it would hardly matter. To make matters worse, Carlos the van driver, elected to take a road involving dozens of speed bumps which he approached by slamming on his brakes just prior to traversing them. I had taken this trip just two weeks prior and don't remember the constant jostling. I crossed my legs, clenched my lower extremities and vowed that I would not be the one to request a *banos* stop.

February 11, 2023 – Huatulco, Mexico. Imagine a knock on your door one morning and, when you answer, 3,000 people stream into your residence but promise to leave by 4 p.m.

That's what the natives must feel like when a cruise ship pulls into port.

Just the sight of this cavernous vessel changes the whole look and feel of towns like Huatulco, nestled in the state of Oaxaca, on the country's Pacific Coast. Looking at it from the beach, it appears as if a skyscraper collapsed into the ocean and recovery ships towed it to the dock and tied it up.

I was feeling especially lonely today. As a result, I got off the ship, wandered over to the Holiday Inn and inquired "Beach?" to the front desk attendant. He wrote down the names of two beaches, Playa La Entrege and Maguey Bay but that was the extent of his English. Another employee suggested I try Maguey because, after I said "food?" she nodded in agreement.

A taxi pulled up and I pointed to the word "Maguey" which had been written on the paper. Off we went, the cab driver operating a stick shift over rough terrain and me wondering if I would eventually be found dismembered in a trunk.

My confidence in my driver grew when he deposited me unharmed, at Maguey Bay. I gestured to my watch and said "Tres?" meaning "Pick me up at 3 p.m.?" He held up three fingers, signifying that he understood.

I've always been fascinated that in some countries, cab drivers will offer to pick you up at a later time in the exact same spot where they dropped you off. Furthermore, they keep their word. This would never happen in the United States. Imagine telling a cab driver "Look, I've got a meeting in this building, but it should be done in two hours. Can you swing by at 1 p.m.?" The driver might agree but all bets are off if he gets a better fare.

Having the same driver for both drop off and pick up duties has served me well over the years, as I am prone to leaving items in taxis. Fifteen minutes after exiting the taxi at Maguey, I realized my Airpods were missing. I remembered shoving them into my bathing suit pocket before leaving my cabin and assumed they were gone forever. I even searched "Airpods" on Amazon while laying on the hot sand, so certain was I that I was out $200 due to carelessness.

At PRECISELY, 3 p.m. my driver appeared in a turnaround lane dotted with other cabs. I got in and immediately saw a set of Airpods sitting on his transom. Gesturing, I said "Are those mine?"

"Si," came the reply.

I tipped him 15 pesos.

February 12, 2023 – Somewhere near Puerto Vallarta. In the health club today, I saw a passenger with a small "FUCK YOU" tattoo on the back of his right ankle. And I thought, "If you're that angry, wouldn't you want that tattoo to have greater visibility?"

This was two days after I noticed another passenger wearing a T-shirt with lengthy verbiage on it. All I noticed though were the first three words: "Guns Kill People." I immediately liked the guy. Then he moved slightly, and I noticed the first word in that sentence was "If."

I immediately hated him.

February 15, 2023 – Chicago, IL. Today I found myself in a drug store contemplating whether to purchase bar soap or liquid "hair and body wash." I opted for the former, surmising that a product that washes your hair and one that cleans your ass should not be sold in the same package.

February 23, 2023 – Washington DC. Today I was speaking at the Gaylord National Harbor Hotel, which has the distinction of being the only hotel in our nation's capital that is inaccessible by means other than an outlandishly priced taxi or Uber ride. I've always been a fan of public rail transportation; despite the consistent smell of urine, and the fear that one sneeze by a fellow rider could put me in the hospital, it's the most convenient and economical way to get around a city. The Washington DC Metro is, hands down, my favorite rail system as it's quiet, relatively odor free and will drop you close to any tourist attraction or place of lodging…with the exception of the National Harbor Hotel.

Blame the Gaylord for their zeal in building hotels that are close to, well, nothing. I've stayed at Gaylord properties in Nashville, Orlando, San Antonio and Washington; all the hotels are amazing if you never plan to leave. I've been to cities that don't have the population of Nashville's Opryland, nor the confusing layout. During my first booking there, I actually got lost going to the ballroom where I was to perform, never mind that I had visited it several hours before for sound check. I have since learned to look at landmarks as I make my way to the elevators, never again wanting to be confused and apprehensive so close to show time.

After checking into Harborside, I discovered the hotel would, the following week, be the site of the annual CPAC convention, featuring a cavalcade of far-right wing legislators and an audience of nutjobs who feel Donald Trump should be president for life.

Following my show, I would have paid whatever fare Uber calculated just to be the hell away from there.

March 8, 2023 – Denver, CO. I went for a late afternoon walk along the 18th Street mall and heard a male voice say "Hey, we know you." I looked and saw three men, all wearing T-shirts emblazoned with the single word "FOCUS," the theme of the meeting I had just attended as the closing keynote speaker. The company specialized in apartment management and real estate investment and these three were employees and audience members.

They were also passing a joint back and forth.

"We heard the jokes man," said one, referring to the observations I had delivered about the cannabis trade in Colorado. I have concluded that everyone in The Golden State is really high but also really healthy. That's the setup. The punch line is telling the audience a man once took exception to that observation, approached me and said "Hey, I have lived in Colorado my entire life. We are NOT all healthy."

"You know you want some dude," he said, holding out a half-completed pre-rolled joint that, in Colorado, is as accessible as a Starbucks latte.

I often drink post show with audience members but, even after 25 years in the business, could never recall getting stoned with one. And yet, show completed and with another evening alone in a strange city to contemplate, it seemed harmless. I took a medium sized hit, thanked them for their generosity and continued my walk.

Thirty minutes later, the weed now fully functioning, I found the lone empty chair at some non-descript brewpub. Seated next to me was another male solo traveler, in his mid-50s, employed by United Airlines and, coincidentally, from Chicago. What started as a congenial conversation quickly devolved as I realized this guy was off the charts annoying. I asked if he had kids; he affirmed that he had three, ages 18, four and two. He then showed me pictures of two dogs and a bird, the latter perched on his shoulder. "My kids," he said proudly.

As I gulped my beer, anxious to leave and find somewhere, anywhere, to have a conversation with someone, anyone, less self-absorbed, he revealed he'd once been kicked out of a bar on a previous company trip to Denver. He neglected to reveal the establishment's name. I wished I were there simply because he would not have been among the patrons.

"For what?" I said.

"For singing some obnoxious Christmas songs," he said before launching into the following:

"Dashing through the bar
Trying to get laid
Looking for some puss…"

"Okay, no need to finish," I said as he laughed.

However, upon hearing I was a comedian, he told me a joke that had me genuinely laughing:

"What's the difference between a Carnival cruise ship and a trailer park?

When one's full, the other's empty."

All in all, not a bad evening.

March 9, 2023 – Chicago, IL. Bruce Springsteen is touring the country and based on my social media feeds, I am the country's only person who doesn't have a ticket.

Perhaps it's because during divorce proceedings, every expenditure gets equated to lawyer's fees. For example, I could spend $350 for main floor Springsteen seats or I could pay my lawyer one hour of time for him to send me emails with subject lines like "Balance Due."

I've seen the Boss twice, but the last time was 1985 on the Born in the USA tour and I haven't been back for various reasons. However, I do possess something that many of my Springsteen-obsessed friends would drool over; a selfie with Bruce, taken after he visited a select number of bookstores around the country to promote his autobiography, aptly titled *Born to Run.*

For the price of the book, and a willingness to continue hitting "refresh" on my computer when tickets to the signing became available, I was one of 1500 people who cued up in horrible November Chicago weather to rub shoulders with rock and roll immortality for upwards of 10 seconds, and leave with multiple photos of the two of us taken with our cell phones by a member of Springsteen's entourage.

I arrived two hours before Springsteen and got in line behind Jean Ann, who had seen Springsteen dozens of times and was only too happy to recount each performance. Telling fans like Jean Ann that I had only seen two Springsteen shows was like eating one M&M at a chocolate convention.

I also told her my strategy for meeting famous people; basically to come up with a question or a comment they have never heard before. It's an excellent tactic but, as someone who has interviewed many celebrities, I also know they have multiple "canned" answers that they use, no matter the question. Months before he became

Johnny Carson's permanent replacement, I interviewed Jay Leno by phone. I could have asked him whether he'd ever slept with any 10-year-old girls and his response would have been "Ya know, I just like to tell jokes."

But as I told Jean Ann, I had a plan for Springsteen. Months before his bookstore appearance, I had written a column on the Boss's penchant for crowd surfing during his shows, something you wouldn't expect from a rocker in his mid-60s at the time. I dubbed the ritual the "Springsteen workout" and vowed, during the column, to get myself into that kind of shape.

When I was in the "on-deck circle" to meet Springsteen, I surrendered my phone. Approaching him, I extended my hand and said "Hey Bruce, Greg Schwem from the Chicago Tribune. I wrote about…"

He cut me off. "Cool man," he said, taking my hand and pivoting us both toward the attendant holding my phone, who had already begun snapping.

And then it was over. My original, witty introduction was ignored, and I exited the stage. I suppose that if I had to shake 1500 hands and pose for 1500 pictures in one day, I would probably ignore everyone as well. I would also dive, headfirst, into a pool of hand sanitizer that evening.

I messaged Jean Ann that afternoon, as we had become Facebook friends while standing in line. "What did you say to him?" I asked.

"Oh, just that I loved him," she said.

Not as original but, I'm sure, a similar outcome.

March 11, 2023 – Chicago, IL. Today was Chicago's annual St. Patrick's Day celebration, a chance for hundreds of thousands of inebriated individuals to marvel at how a river can turn bright green seconds after being laced with a powdery substance which, believe it or not, is bright orange.

The celebration also features a parade which is a chance for every Chicago union member to help assemble a float and then march, inebriated, down Columbus Drive. Parades in Chicago last the equivalent of Netflix TV series; I attended the 2022 Gay Pride parade, which ended about the same time entrants were lining up for the 2023 event. Upon reaching the finish line, some participants just returned to their original start positions and waited.

In honor of St. Patrick's Day, I will now share my favorite Irish limerick:

There once was a man from Kildaire
Making love to his wife on the stairs
He was on his last stroke,
When the banister broke,
So he finished her off in mid air.

March 20, 2023 – Chicago, IL. While transitioning to city living, I have been dabbling in taking public transportation to both of Chicago's airports, an experiment that might cause me to reconsider early morning flights. Like most major cities, Chicago has a horrible and sad homeless problem. Public transit provides temporary shelter and, in bone chilling conditions, warmth.

Such was the case while taking the red, and then the blue line to O'Hare airport at 5:15 a.m. Upon entering the subway I realized I was the only passenger accompanied by luggage. Three men and a woman walked back and forth, with the woman mumbling about being a "disciple."

One of the men, clad in a Blackhawks Stanley Cup championship jacket, replied "Do you know what a disciple is?"

"I'm a disciple of Bobby Rush," she said, referring to the former U.S. representative from Illinois' first district. She then vomited a cherry looking substance next to a trash receptacle.

The train arrived shortly thereafter.

Changing trains at State and Lake Street did not yield better company. I entered the car and realized it was just myself and one other rider. He was talking very loudly about topics ranging from Donald Trump to "the bitch who left me" to "smackin' the shit out of that guy." Upon seeing me, he decided to change seats, right next to me. I silently thanked Apple for inventing Airpods.

However, just before increasing the volume, I heard him say "Stop me if you've heard this one before."

I turned off the music. "Is this guy homeless?" I thought. "Or is he trying out material? Maybe we worked together at an open mic night."

I kept listening, waiting for a pause in his ranting so I could say, "Go back to the part about the bitch leaving you. I might have a tag for that bit."

April 6, 2023 – Somewhere off the coast of Montenegro. For the last five days, I have been on a cruise ship with a collection of passengers who have spent the last 90 days living together and plan to continue doing so for at least another 22.

I am ready to jump overboard after six.

The group has decided to traverse the world, literally, aboard the Island Princess. Round the world cruises are becoming quite popular, with multiple lines offering them and the itineraries becoming lengthier until, I feel, one line will add a day in space providing everyone can be back on board by early dinner seating.

This group left from Long Beach California on January 19, headed west and never looked back. Along the way, they visited the Hawaiian Islands, continued to New Zealand and Australia, overnighted in Phuket, Thailand, spent 12 hours in Sri Lanka, photographed the Suez Canal, and managed to squeeze in a day in Gythion, Greece before I joined. They had to skirt ports for reasons ranging from "rough seas" to "political unrest;" indeed, choppy waters forced the captain to turn away from Koper, Slovenia and Split, Croatia, while I was aboard. That was disappointing since I was getting off a week after joining, in Valletta, Malta no less. Without me, the ship's itinerary still included destinations such as Marseille, Marrakesh and the Mexican Riviera before arriving back in Long Beach on May 11. All this for a starting price of just under $20,000. When I joined, the captain had just been replaced. How long a cruise is it when the passengers outlast the guy driving the vessel?

They were an odd bunch; something I learned a few days after boarding in Ravenna, Italy, day 75 of the cruise. At first, I thought I had hit the jackpot regarding my goal to meet as many interesting people, post-divorce, as possible. The sights they have already seen and the stories they can tell would know no bounds. That was certainly the case when I chatted up a few passengers on a shuttle operating between the ship and downtown Ravenna. Connie was from California, traveling solo and had saved up for three years to make the journey.

Jamie was from Las Vegas and so claustrophobic that she had to sit directly behind the bus's middle exit door. She spent the whole ride plotting her escape the moment the ride ended. She and her husband Nick at one time owned a mobile home park. Claustrophobia, incidentally, is not an ideal malady to suffer from if planning to live in a cruise cabin for four months. The old "I can sit on the toilet and shave, shower and shit" joke endures to this day.

"I could talk to these people for hours," I thought as they regaled me with tales of purchasing camera equipment in Turkey and feeling ill in Jordan.

Except they didn't want to talk to me. At times I felt like I was a college student who transferred mid-semester and everybody in the dorm had already found their friend groups. They were polite enough during my show, laughing but not uproariously laughing as so many cruise ship audiences are prone to do, simply because they are on vacation. Then again, when you've already seen Dubai, how excited are you going to be by a comedian?

Many, like Connie, were alone. Others were with their spouses but talked little during meals. I began wondering if they were on the ship to improve their marriages? Or if they thought their relationships were so solid that nothing, not even political coups in unpronounceable cities, could cause breakdowns? Maybe they had just run out of things to talk about so why not see the world as opposed to conversing?

The night after my performance, I wandered into the showroom to watch a guy named Chris Ritchie, whose show was entitled "I am Diamond, Brooklyn Born & Raised."

It was a long-winded way to say he was a Neil Diamond impersonator.

I couldn't tell if Ritchie was an impersonator who just had a gift for mimicking a particular celebrity, exercised that gift for an hour a night and then reverted to a normal personality for the rest of the day OR whether he actually thought he was Diamond and never wanted to drop the act, so to speak.

After watching him warble through "I Am, I Said" and address the audience in his best Diamond non-singing voice, I chose the latter. Maybe I'm cynical because I loathe cover bands and cover singers for not creating their own art, but simply replicating somebody else's. It doesn't work that way for comedians. Ritchie closes with "Sweet Caroline" and has the audience singing "So good, so good, so good" every time he belts out "Good times never seemed so good." If I closed with a Jerry Seinfeld bit, it would be the last time I worked that particular venue.

I never saw Ritchie around the ship but I assume he spent most of the time in his cabin, ironing his wig.

It was also the moment I decided I had enough material for a book.

"When I was a kid my parents moved a lot, but I always found them."

– Attributed to Rodney Dangerfield (BrainyMedia 2024)

E) Unpack Everything Quickly...So You Have More Time to Wait

Shawshank Redemption, my favorite prison movie and far ahead of *Escape from Alcatraz* features a touching scene with James Whitmore, who plays career convict Brooks. After spending most of his life behind the prison's walls and finally being granted parole, we see Brooks amazed, and terrified, of the outside world he tries to navigate.

Clad in a suit and tie, he fearfully clutches the forward seat of a city bus, appearing unsure of its destination or when he needs to exit. Attempting to cross a street on foot, he nearly gets run over before quickening his pace.

"I saw an automobile once when I was a kid but now, they're everywhere," he recounts in a letter to Andy, Red and his other friends back at Shawshank.

"I don't like it here…I've decided not to stay," he continues before hanging himself in the boarding house that was his new home, free of bars, head counts and sadistic guards. (Darabont 1994)

I saw similarities in myself and Brooks' situations, even though I only briefly thought about not "staying." It's painful to admit suicidal thoughts but I think you'd be hard pressed to find an individual who doesn't, even for a moment, contemplate ending it all when life is closing in due to a decision that, at the time, seemed so right. In 2017, Joe, a successful financial trader and one of my tennis and golf partners, hung himself in his bedroom closet after discovering a warrant had been issued for his arrest. The charges stemmed from his behavior during divorce proceedings.

When we choose divorce, we tend to think only of the positives; freedoms we didn't think we had before, the chance to finally, put ourselves first as opposed to our spouse, our kids, our pets. The list goes on and on.

We are so anxious to begin our new lives that in so doing, we forget some of the conveniences we had in the old ones. While I made the money, my wife handled the finances and ensured bills were paid on time. Now I had to do that, and it didn't take long before a credit card company slapped me with a late fee for doing it poorly.

For years we employed a cleaning service consisting of two or three Polish-speaking ladies who arrived every other Tuesday, stayed for four hours and, amazingly, managed to clean a four-bedroom house in that time. This was AFTER they had completed cleaning the house next door, which was even larger.

I didn't know how to unclog a vacuum. I didn't even OWN a vacuum.

Assembling furniture, dealing with medical insurers, determining whether refrigerator items were spoiled or still "reasonably safe" were all events that became part of my day planner once I decided to move out, but one could hardly term it a prison, at least not figuratively. I had a comfortable home, one warm in the winter and cool in the summer. I had a lawn sprinkler system that woke me up at 5:30 on summer mornings, the ch-ch-ch sound confirming it was doing its job. I had a BBQ grill and an outdoor stereo system connected to Pandora and Spotify, so I could listen to whatever music I thought set the mood for steak and the beers I consumed while grilling it. I had a car in the garage, a second car in case the first was acting temperamental. I had neighbors who I know would have called the police, or the paramedics, if they sensed my safety or health were in jeopardy.

Is it any wonder that while emitting a steady stream of "FUCK THIS LAMP AND FUCK THE IDIOTS WHO THINK IT CAN BE ASSEMBLED WITH A FUCKING ALLEN WRENCH!" I stopped and thought, "What have I done?"

But I'd done it. Just as my ex had. We'd agreed there were irreconcilable differences and signed the legal documents confirming it. We were 50 percent responsible for what lie ahead. It was confusing. But when I'm confused, I tend to laugh. And that's what I vowed to do, beginning on the day that I hired a moving company called "College Hunks" to remove my belongings from a storage facility and transport them to a dwelling where the sounds of sprinklers were replaced with sirens (hopefully not preceded by gunshots) and a cleaning service that consisted of…me.

Incidentally, "College Hunks" is a bit misleading of a title for the dudes who showed up at my facility. Only one looked, in my eyes anyway, to have "hunk" potential and I'm not sure any of the three ever attended college. But they came armed with leather straps, furniture pads and a truck. That was good enough for me.

A self-storage facility may be the most depressing place on earth, apart from an Amazon warehouse, covered in a later chapter. Beginning one's divorce by first determining whether all your contents can fit into a 10x10 unit or you need to spring for four feet of additional length simply adds to the mood. How can anybody make that determination, while a self-storage sales associated stands there offering no help or advice? Then again, what would Marge, my associate, have said? It's not like she was a realtor, eager to point out features such as walk-in closets, floor-to-ceiling views and good school systems. She was selling me space, nothing more.

I think you're really going to like this one Greg. The cement floor is free of stains and this sliding metal door is easy to unlock, ensuring you can open the unit pain free, and become more depressed at your situation. I've got three other offers on this baby, so I wouldn't wait.

Actually, she did tell me others were interested in the unit and it might not be available by this time tomorrow. I gave her a deposit.

Everybody entering or leaving a storage facility is miserable. Or pissed. Or both. I had my belongings in a unit for six weeks and, whenever I paid them a visit, I never encountered a fellow renter whose expression said, "There is NOTHING I would rather do on this glorious day than move shit to and from my van while questioning why I even need most of it."

They have dropped money at this depressing combination of loading docks, elevators, hallways and identical looking garage doors, for one of three reasons:

1) Like me, they are in transition between residences

2) They are having difficulty downsizing or, worse, have a serious hoarding addiction
3) They are looking to dispose of evidence from the crime they just committed

Storage facility owners know this but, with the possible exception of number three, don't care. In 2011 I delivered a motivational comedic keynote address for employees of Public Storage, the granddaddy of self-storage companies. It included an in-person meeting with executives who, I determined, felt almost guilty about their business, specifically the fact that they were *encouraging* people to hold onto shit they really should have hauled to a landfill. It was like selling cigarettes to teenagers or standing outside an AA meeting with a new flavor of Patron.

True to my vow of always trying to find something to laugh at, no matter the situation, I began observing the items others were moving, and trying to figure out what role said items had played in the owners' past and future lives. I do the same thing at grocery stores, peering into shoppers' carts and assessing why certain items were purchased. I'm still flummoxed by the guy, three years ago, whose cart contained a jumbo pack of diapers and a 12-pack of beer. Was he a stay-at-home dad eager, I mean REALLY eager, to reward himself when his wife returned from a business trip? Was he the lifelong single uncle who thought "How difficult can this baby-sitting thing be?" Or something in between?

Or, more recently, the attractive woman, mid-30s, purchasing a laxative and a large bouquet of flowers. What was her deal? Did she seek something pleasant to look at while the laxative did its due diligence? Did she feel the need to fill her house with fragrance for obvious reasons? Was her uncooperative digestive system keeping her from her love of gardening? The possibilities were endless.

Playing this game in storage facilities can be even more entertaining.

On my first visit, after unloading 15 boxes from a rickety cart into my unit and realizing months of physical therapy was in my near future, I exited the elevator to find a gentleman with two items on his cart: a truck tire and an electronic piano keyboard.

My mind did not even know where to begin.

Was he part of a musical group called "Spare Automotive Parts"? It was plausible. Or was there a disabled tour bus stranded somewhere and this guy was elected to find a replacement tire while ditching the one that had just run over a sharp object? That seemed far-fetched; why take the keyboard on this mission? That task seemed more suited for the bass player.

I longed to ask his intentions, but I chose to remain silent. Nobody in a storage facility wants to chat, because as previously noted, nobody in a storage facility is in a pleasant mood.

On my next trip, this time to OPEN all the boxes until I found some important tax documents I had inadvertently packed, I shared an elevator with a couple whose cart contained two paintings and an industrial sized bag of dog food. I'm no art aficionado, so I couldn't critique the paintings' subject matter or artistic styles. I chose to focus on the dog food.

Were these two planning to paint a ravenous canine? Or did they just need something to keep their own pet occupied while they plied their craft? Judging from the size of the bag, the latter scenario meant the pair were notoriously slow painters.

Perhaps they weren't artists at all but merely art collectors. I imagined the couple, their dog between them, gazing at their latest purchase in the foyer of their expensive home. They would celebrate with a succulent dinner of red wine, two steaks cooked medium rare and grain free kibble. Music would be all that was lacking.

I know of a keyboard player who could fit the bill. Although he may need transportation.

Six weeks after the hunks moved everything to my unit, they returned to empty it and relocate my possessions to a 14th floor condominium on Chicago's north side. The neighborhood contained, in my opinion, everything my old environment lacked; restaurants with unpronounceable names, jogging and bike trails that didn't require jogging or biking to locate, residents who stayed awake past 8 p.m. and an energy that I had never experienced during early morning walks with my dog or evening trips to my suburban "downtown" which consisted of three decent restaurants, all of which were hopelessly packed on weekends.

Those were the plusses.

The minuses of my "hood" included a grocery store that, while walkable, featured aisles too thin for grocery carts to pass in opposite directions. Trust me, road rage has nothing on "cart rage" particularly when one of those carts is piloted by an elderly female who felt this neighborhood began deteriorating in 1979 and got even worse when all the "millenniums" started moving in.

My neighborhood also lacked quiet.

Living a block from Lake Michigan and its accompanying cool breezes meant I rarely needed air conditioning. However, sleeping at night with open windows meant also trying to sleep through piercing sirens, slamming doors, profanity filled breakup arguments (some featuring solely male participants as Chicago's gay community was only three blocks to my west). Living close to a large, alternative-lifestyle community was hardly a deterrent; instead, I found it invigorating just watching people stay true to their feelings, and themselves, without judgement. Events like the city's massive Pride Parade brought together hundreds of thousands of Chicagoans who seemed happy, at least to me. Maybe their attitudes would eventually rub off.

Yes, the city was new, loud and fast paced. My belongings, at least what was left of them, were in the right location. That I was sure of. I left most of the moving cartons unpacked and ventured into the neighborhood, anxious to discover new experiences, hopefully without my own Shawshank moment. Unlike Brooks, I was enjoying a world that "went and got itself in a big damn hurry."

Until I became thirsty.

Stopping in a random bar on Halsted Street, my first destination on my first night as a city dweller, I ordered my standard - a vodka and tonic.

The bartender, young with slicked back hair, two earrings in one ear and a T-shirt featuring some band I'd never heard of, looked as if I'd slapped him.

"We have awesome cocktails here," he said. "Let me make you something and, if you don't like it, I'll make you a vodka and tonic."

"Uh, deal?," I said, not certain what I had agreed to or how much it would cost.

"Any of these sound enticing?" he said, handing me a menu labeled "CRAFT COCKTAILS." I scanned the selections, reading about drinks with ingredients ranging from egg white, to candied ginger to locally sourced honey.

"Surprise me," I said, figuring it was the safest answer. "Just something with vodka in it."

It was as if I'd given him a term paper assignment and told him it needed to be completed in three minutes. Although judging from the assortment of knives, cutting boards, straining utensils and plants that suddenly appeared in front of him, this was no three-minute project.

Soon I learned "craft cocktail" should really be named "20-minute cocktail" and I had better get used to that unless I wished to spend my city existence drinking water, diet coke, beer or any other beverage consisting of a single ingredient.

What happened to cocktail hour? To happy hour? At this pace, happy hour would consist of multiple hours, purely so the bartender could wait on more than one customer. I was writing the dialogue for the bartender as he prepared whatever he insisted I would love.

Good evening, and welcome to The Violet Lily Diamond Club. What can I get you to drink? A Vodka Tonic? Well, I could make you that, but here at VLD we have an extensive CRAFT cocktail menu. May I recommend something a little more bold, edgy and vibrant than the cocktail your parents drank? Great!

In the draft, the font became italics lighter right here. I have fixed it. How about an Afghan saffron horchata? It's made, naturally, with Afghan saffron, green cardamom, vanilla bean, cinnamon, basmati rice, almond, nutmeg and a few other ingredients Noah, our senior mixologist, blended. Trust me, it will be the best Afghan saffron horchata you have ever tasted. I will make the drink right in front of you so you can witness the magic for yourself.

First, I must pulverize the rice and then strain it through this triple-layered cheese cloth using a copper strainer. Some mixologists would skimp and use a stainless steel strainer, but that could lead to graininess; and trust me, there is nothing worse than a grainy horchata! Now stand by while I add evaporated and condensed milk and then stick my finger in the mixture, twirl it ever so slightly and then lick it as if I were Gordon Ramsay.

I'm sorry, I think it needs additional straining.

There, that's perfect. Now it must sit for five minutes in this specially designed refrigerator we purchased purely for storing horchata. But this will give me time to shave down these cinnamon sticks using a spice grinder. Plus I need to separate an egg, as I will need the egg white for extra froth.

By the way, if you're hungry, we do serve food at Violet Lily. Use the QR code. Also, I probably should have asked, but the

Afghan saffron horchata contains tiger nuts. You're not allergic, are you?

Excuse me, I have to run in the back because it appears we are out of vanilla extract.

OK, I'm back. Thank you for your patience. I know it looks like your drink is almost complete, but it's not. We're just teasing you. That's what we do here at Violet Lily. Every time you think you're actually going to get your cocktail, we pull it back because there is another obscure ingredient we will be adding. Why are you looking at your watch? Do you have somewhere to be? Horchatas take a little more time to produce. Heck, we soaked the rice all night just for your sipping pleasure. Please enjoy your loaded nachos in the meantime.

Pardon me, but I must taste again. I'll use a different finger this time.

Hmmmm, definitely needs more orgeat syrup. And the cardamom needs a few minutes to breathe.

Now all I must do is pour everything into this shaker, add a liberal amount of crushed sphere cubes and shake it exactly 375 times. Then I will pour it into this rocks glass and…LIGHT IT ON FIRE. Stand back.

There, it's done! But please wait for it to cool. Horchatas are best served icy cold. So, why did we add an open flame to your cocktail? Because now those two ladies at the end of the bar are intrigued and will probably each want one. That's why we pulverized some extra rice. I just hope we don't run out of green cardamom. One time that happened and, oh how I hate to admit this, we had to substitute BLACK cardamom. We got a two-star Yelp review as a result!

Eight minutes and three glances at my cell phone later, the drink was complete. The bartender pushed it in my direction and this time, didn't retrieve it immediately. Instead, he awaited my review as I took my initial sip.

"It tastes just like a vodka tonic."

That's not what I said but it would have been the truth. Instead, I patted him on the back, figuratively, with the compliment he was waiting for.

"Amazing."

"Glad you like it," he replied. "That will be $18.50. We don't accept cash."

Happiness was going to cause a serious dent in my credit card.

"I never thought it was necessary to own a great deal. The most important thing is to have enough money to have some really good food, buy clothes twice a year and have nice holidays."

– ***John Cleese*** (Das 2024)

F) Foley, Alabama: Here Comes Poor Me

Don't expect anyone to pick up your dinner check in Foley, Alabama.

Nestled at the southern tip of the state served by Senators Tommy "I haven't actually read the Constitution" Tuberville and the now infamous Katie "My kitchen has no appliances" Britt, the city of 22,000-plus was recently named by *Travel + Leisure* magazine as "Best Place to Retire with No Savings." (Leasaca 2024)

That's right, zero, zip, nada. If you don't have an IRA, still don't understand cryptocurrency, had the misfortune of knowing Bernie Madoff, or thought the Mega Millions jackpot in that Vegas casino was "bound to hit eventually," come to Foley.

If you're "runnin' on empty," "chasing chips," "rummaging for rubles" or "trawling for treasure," or have "less dough than a Pizza Hut," head to Foley.

I may soon be joining you.

Mind you, I do have a nest egg, but one that shrunk significantly due to my divorce. Instagram hasn't gotten that message, as my feed is still dotted with ads from investment firms featuring distinguished-looking, gray-haired gentlemen standing outside horse stables (because rich guys own horses, apparently). Accompanying their mugs are thought bubbles with questions like "I'm 60 with $1.2 million in an IRA. Should I convert $120,000 per year to a Roth to avoid required minimum distributions?"

I want to smack these guys so hard they'll need to make hefty withdrawals to cover their dental bills.

Even worse than the guys with the money are the posts from financial advisers telling you what to do with your money, no matter how little you have. You'll find them walking along riverbanks or through autumn foliage saying "If you only have FIVE DOLLARS to invest, here are FIVE THINGS you should do with it."

OK, I'm exaggerating but if these guys are so knowledgeable, what are they doing making videos in the middle of the day? When the markets are open? Shouldn't they be sitting in front of banks of computers, acting on the advice they are freely dishing out to their social media followers? I feel the same way about doctors who've joined the social media advice craze. If a heart attack means I must change my nutritional choices, I want to hear my options from a cardiologist with a schedule packed to the gills. Not from some guy who makes videos entitled "FIVE FOODS NEVER TO KEEP IN YOUR REFRIGERATOR!"

Incidentally, I've watched enough of those to realize all should be retitled "FIVE FOODS GREG SCHWEM ALWAYS KEEPS IN HIS REFRIGERATOR."

Anyway, back to Foley. From its website I learned the town was incorporated in 1915, some 13 years after John Foley, a Chicago boy like me, began buying land to expand railroad service in the area. Today, Foley contains a "historic downtown business district" and "world class attractions" the website boasts. (City of Foley 2024)

All of which certainly require money to enjoy. I mean, how can one shop downtown with a savings account ledger that says zero? Is there a side door in the Foley Railroad Museum allowing one to sneak in and avoid the $4 entrance fee? That money could easily go to rent!

Luckily, Foley housing seems fairly affordable with rents averaging $840 per month between 2017 and 2021 and the median value of homes around $205,000 according to the website.

Also, there are plenty of free activities. Just ask Guy Busby, the city's marketing and communication manager and a Foley-area resident for more than 30 years.

"We're only about 11 miles from Gulf Shores," he said, referring to the Alabama resort town where, I assume, it's free to throw a towel on the sand and spend all day staring at the Gulf of Mexico while contemplating your bad financial decisions. (Schwem 2024) If I packed my own lunch and commandeered an abandoned beach chair, I could probably return to my Foley domicile even, or just slightly in the red.

Busby also recommended the 500-acre Graham Creek Nature Reserve, Foley's springtime concert and movie series, and the recently renovated $1.2 million Sara Thompson Kids Park, True. nearly half the park's cost was offset by grants but the price tag shows that somebody in Foley has bucks.

He also mentioned the Tropic Falls at OWA water park, but I don't think that's going to happen. I took my kids to loads of water parks in their youth and, at day's end, the only thing dry was my wallet's interior. Corn dogs, greasy pizza and beer (Dad's treat for suffering through a day at a water park) aren't getting any cheaper.

Maybe I'll move to Foley and take on a side hustle for extra income. There's something enticing about driving for Uber, as I doubt I would encounter the traffic congestion in Foley that one finds in Chicago. Plenty of snowbirds and tourists visit the city, Busby said, and they'll certainly need transportation, as well as recommendations from a "local" like me. I will welcome them into my (hopefully) paid-off vehicle, introduce myself and tell them there is only one rule they must abide by.

Cash up front.

"I quit therapy because my analyst was trying to help me behind my back."

– ***Richard Lewis*** (Heller 2020)

G) I Don't Need a Good Therapist. Just an Available One

There are currently 7.8 billion people roaming this earth of which, by my own estimates, 7.7 billion are in therapy.

Which explains why I cannot find a therapist.

I had resisted the temptation to spill my guts about my situation to an independent third party despite pleadings from friends, relatives and even my attorney. My pig-headed response never wavered:

"My therapy is knowing I am getting divorced. My therapy will end the day the divorce is final."

Besides, I had a relative who was a licensed marriage and family therapist. From the time I moved out, I would occasionally bounce my issues off her although I was careful not to call or text her at all hours of the day with my crises. Still, it was an ace in my back pocket and it felt good. I've often heard that every extended family should have at least one lawyer, one accountant, one car mechanic and one computer whiz. In this screwed up world we live in I'd add "therapist" to that list.

At least one of my family members is in therapy, maybe more. My friends are in therapy; their kids are in therapy. Your kids' teacher is in therapy. Your Pilates instructor is in therapy. So are your retired parents. At least three-quarters of my stand-up comedian friends begin their sets with "So I was talking with my therapist…"

Therapists are in therapy. Just ask Lori Gottlieb, an LA-based therapist and author of the best-seller *Maybe You Should Talk to Someone.* Gottlieb sought help after a painful breakup with her boyfriend, a man she erroneously thought would eventually become her husband and a father to her son. Gottlieb pioneered her book into an advice column, a podcast and probably a multi-part Netflix series. I'm guessing she is worth more money than some of the Hollywood clients she hints at in her book.

Prior to taking the therapy plunge, I borrowed Gottlieb's book from my local library but only because I thought maybe her insights into why people seek therapy and what they can expect, could solve my issues. Maybe I wouldn't need a therapist after all! I had to place a hold on the book, but a two-week wait was more appealing than $150 an hour.

It was an entertaining and insightful read but, unfortunately, didn't provide closure. Time to visit the ATM!

Therapists come in all shapes and sizes. Gottlieb is pretty and petite; I found an image of her standing next to Oprah Winfrey and the talk show queen looked positively gargantuan standing next to her. Was Gottlieb counseling Oprah? No clue.

Then there was John Kim, author of the best seller *Single On Purpose: Redefine Everything. Find Yourself First.* A Korean-American with wildly-flowing gray hair and a bevy of tattoos, Kim looked like he would easily beat the shit out of any patient not following his advice. No wonder his book stemmed from a blog entitled "The Angry Therapist."

Dr. Phil fell somewhere in between. Yes, I listened to some of his podcasts as well.

Google "therapy statistics" and the first results invariably address Gen Z and Millennials, who have embraced therapy the way mosquitos embrace a picnic. The Thriving Center of Psychology, an online mental health platform, surveyed 1,099 members of these demographics – note, it would have been an even 1,100 but the last participant scored an emergency therapy session that day - and found that in 2024, 39 percent planned to put "therapy appointment" in their day planners. (Thriving Center of Psych 2023) Anxiety and depression were the most common reasons but rounding out the top 10 were stress, desire for personal growth, trauma, ADHD, life transitions, sleep problems, relationship troubles and loneliness. Of the top 30 U.S. cities searching for therapists, or just seeking answers about mental health, Baltimore was number one followed by Denver, Seattle, Portland and Las Vegas. Shockingly, Los Angeles was last. I say shockingly because that's the city most in need of therapy. Unless thousands of struggling actors and actresses suddenly up and moved to Baltimore.

Chicago was 23. Personally, I think Chicago is as fucked up as any other city; we just can't make it to therapy five months out of the year because subfreezing temperatures have killed our car batteries.

College-aged kids, whatever you are currently majoring in, drop it and switch to a major that requires a sympathetic ear and an office with comfy couches and chairs. Well, I'm not sure about the latter; there may be some New Age or "edgy" therapists out there who feel clients are at their most vulnerable or open when engaged in wall squats. Or dialing into a Zoom session while standing at one of those motorized desks that changes heights with the press of a button. Prior to seeking professional help, I'd only seen the office of one therapist, a college friend and licensed psychiatrist. I also spent a good amount of time in his waiting room, as his final appointment of the day went long, delaying our dinner plans.

If you have always aspired to be a therapist be advised a good portion of your day will be spent answering emails with a curt "I'm sorry, but I'm not accepting new patients/clients/cases. May I recommend (insert name of equally overbooked colleague)?" Therapists must answer these electronic cries for help because their websites fail to mention their bulging calendars. Instead, potential clients are invited to fill out forms stating why they need professional help, lulling them into false senses of hope in the process.

Incidentally, even my college friend is booked. So much so that the offer of dinner at a restaurant of his choice couldn't free up a spot on his calendar.

One therapist limited his queries to 200 words. Seriously? How does one condense a failed marriage of 29 years into 200 words? And yet I thought, maybe succinctly defining my issues, instead of rambling on about my childhood, my marriage, my physical health and my current mental state, might be a good exercise. Why not drill down now as opposed to when I was on the couch and the meter was running?

I reworked my query, shortening sentences and thoughts whenever possible. It didn't matter, as his response required only four words: "My calendar is full."

As any therapist will admit, COVID is the reason for this mental health crisis. Discussing your problems with strangers suddenly became more popular, and chic, than online wine tastings. Kids unable to deal with virtual school ran to therapists. Couples, suddenly living under the same roof 24 hours a day, sought therapy. Moms and dads, worried about how virtual school was affecting their children, sent them to therapy.

We all suffered from isolation.

Therapists became the answer, even if we had to meet with them while isolated. Shortly after opening my Google Search channels, I did find a therapist who offered me a virtual or "telehealth" session, but I declined. One nugget I gleaned from Gottlieb's book, for both patient and therapist, is that face-to-face interaction is far more successful, and gratifying, than Zoom sessions. You don't have to tell me that. Remember, during COVD I did Zoom comedy for two years.

Two weeks after sounding the alarm, I heard from a therapist I'll call Grant, who offered to see me the next week. Grant had not just one time slot available, but several, leading me to think this guy must really suck at his craft. Or maybe he was spending all his time making TikTok videos. Still, beggars can't be choosers. I consented, verified his sessions were covered under my wife's insurance plan and, a week later, found myself standing outside a non-descript three story office building bordering a Chicago Metra rail line. I was stoked that Grant's office was only about two miles from my condo and accessible by bike should I choose.

For my first session, the weather was too cold and miserable for a bike ride, so I parked on a residential street and, per Grant's instructions, entered his private code and waited to be buzzed in.

A flight of stairs awaited me. At the top was, ironically, a bike storage room. Lotta avid cyclists in therapy, I decided. Turning right, I encountered Grant's waiting room, which doubled as the employee break room. A refrigerator and Keurig coffee machine were available. I was never alone; there was always at least one other person sitting on one of the plastic chairs, usually scrolling furiously through his or her phone, and waiting to be greeted by another therapist. It was obvious multiple therapists shared this space. I tried not to stare at my therapy companions but couldn't help wondering what issues were bedeviling their lives and would they feel any better an hour from now?

Children particularly intrigued me. What could possibly be bothering the eight-year-old girl who emerged from a session to her beaming mother, who asked "Was today a GOOD day?"

An approving nod from the girl's therapist seemed to confirm it was.

Or the four-year-old boy, fidgeting on the chair and engrossed in his mom's iPhone until his therapist emerged and asked if he was "ready to talk?" The boy immediately took the phone and retreated under a nearby chair, forcing the therapist to lower herself to his level and bargain with him.

"How about your mom takes the phone and you get to see all these cool new 'Transformer' toys I have?"

Surprisingly, to me anyway, the boy relented.

Were these kids really that fucked up at such early ages? Or did their parents just make that decision for them and wanted an outsider to not only confirm their diagnosis, but do something about it?

Eventually Grant entered the kitchen, introduced himself and motioned for me to follow him. My first thought, not that it mattered, was how short he was. Five four and some change. It would be like opening my soul to my little brother if I had one.

Sitting on a couch opposite Grant's chair I talked for most of the first session, as I imagine most patients do when finally landing a therapy appointment. I probably could have spent the hour recounting how difficult it was to book an appointment. I didn't feel like a "patient," despite the label therapists give to those seeking counseling. That feeling is reserved for when I'm sitting on a sheet of tissue, in an always too cold examining room, waiting for a doctor to insert an equally cold finger into my ass and feel my prostate. At least Grant's office was warmer.

While I blathered on about my marital history, my pre-marital history, and all history in between, Grant listened, never once making notes nor recording the conversation. I found that odd but reasoned he either didn't find it necessary or had a prodigious memory. Occasionally he would interrupt, long enough to utter one of the following phrases:

1) "Makes sense"

2) "Agree"
3) "Sure, I can see that"

Just as I was about to say "are you sure you're getting all this?" the session was over. I had cried once, said "fuck" half a dozen times (I was counting even if Grant wasn't), made Grant laugh twice (hey, I'm a comedian; it's in my blood) and admitted to shortcomings and confusion in areas ranging from communication to sexual fantasies. I'm sure it was nothing Grant hadn't heard before, at least in some capacity. I left wondering what revelations would cause a therapist to stop saying "agree" and say "Wait, WHAT did you just say?"

I am still wondering.

I liked Grant enough to make another appointment, ten days later. This time, as we delved deeper into why my marriage had fallen apart, I decided this session was going to be a two-way conversation, one void of monosyllabic responses from Grant. At various points I would stop and wait for him to react or offer advice on something I said.

Rarely did anything emerge from his mouth. It was like playing a game of "chicken" with him. Who would break the silence first?

It was then I began wondering if therapy was right for me, at least at this point in my journey to becoming a divorced man. I made a third appointment but, after feeling nothing, told Grant I didn't think I was his ideal client, patient, customer, mortgage payor or whatever he chose to call me. I could have cited the Thriving Center for Psychology Statistics, which said most people seeking therapy visit at least two therapists before making a choice.

At the same time I was dumping Grant, I had become more immersed in Kim's book *Single On Purpose.* Recommended to me by a lifelong single friend, the book stressed how difficult it was to be suddenly single when you'd never really been single. It was like reading my autobiography. Solitude, at least in my home environment, was something I'd never experienced. After college, I had always had roommates right up until the time I met my wife, where I exchanged a male to share the rent with, for a wife to share, well, everything with.

And now to divide everything with.

Being suddenly single was difficult Kim said, but not impossible. Not if one learned to find communities formed by people with similar interests and engage with strangers in public settings as opposed to disappearing in one's phone, alone. All of this was part of the longer-term goal of making new friends, something that was easy at 10 but not at 60.

In the next section, I will cover how I had already begun the process of trying new endeavors. I just hadn't considered any of them to be social in nature, or ones that would lead to friendships. That would eventually change.

Act II
THE REINVENTION

"Most people work just hard enough not to get fired and get paid just enough money not to quit."

– Attributed to George Carlin (BrainyMedia 2024)

H) Side Hustle #1 – I'm Sorry Your Amazon Gift Went to St. Kitts Instead of St. Louis

I spent my first day at Amazon staring at my new coworkers' shoes.

One requirement of working in an Amazon warehouse is possessing steel-toed footwear. That's never been part of a comedian's wardrobe although there have been a few audience members I would have gladly kicked following performances, relishing the chance to alter their chatty, insulting mouths, and accompanying dental work, with a hard metal alloy.

Amazon provides new employees with $110 vouchers for purchasing shoes from Zappos.com, an online clothing store that also sells stylish men's bomber jackets. I would have preferred spending my voucher on one of those as, soon-to-be-single, it may have attracted interest from female co-workers.

Who's the leather-clad guy hauling that pallet? Yowza!

Instead, I purchased a pair of black/blue Reebok Work Speed TR Work EH Comp Toe, size 10. After slipping them on, I had an overwhelming urge to go bowling.

I have been hired as an Amazon "sortation center warehouse associate" at the company's Crest Hill, Illinois fulfilment center. When you suddenly find yourself alone, lonely and with time on your hands, you long for conversation, new experiences or anything that can, even momentarily, transport you into situations where you don't have to think about lawyers, relationships, sadness or mistakes you made that precipitated all three. At least I did. Which is why I decided to explore the ranks of "gig workers" in the "gig economy," a term coined in 2009 by journalist Tina Brown. Writing for *The Daily Beast* at the time, Brown described a workforce full of freelance employees who stitched together "a bunch of free-floating projects, consultancies and part-time bits and pieces while they transacted in a digital marketplace." (Brown 2009)

Eight years later, updating that piece, Brown herself seemed amazed at what her term had morphed into.

"With so many part-time people on—and not on—the job, corporate America has started to feel like it's on a permanent maternity leave," Brown wrote. "Colleagues are an amorphous, free-floating army of rotating waifs whose voicemails are clogged with plaintive requests from their own offices for missing information."

Brown apparently is enamored with the term "free floating."

I consider myself neither amorphous, a waif or a free-floater but that didn't stop me from being curious about gig work. I leaned into it not for financial benefit although extra income is always nice, no matter your monetary status. If a millionaire finds a 20-dollar bill on the street, he will pocket it. His day just improved. He may even recount the story to fellow millionaires at his private club that evening. They will be envious.

My youngest daughter actually beat me to gig work. Prior to my wife and I separating, she decided to make her newly purchased car her summer office. One day she casually informed me she was now a food delivery driver for DoorDash. Her job consisted of picking up food orders from various local restaurants, fast food establishments and coffee bars and driving them to hungry people too self-absorbed and, by their own standards, too busy to walk to the corner Starbucks. I honestly don't believe Starbucks will consider itself a successful franchise until there actually IS a Starbucks on every corner. At last count, there are only about 37 corners left to conquer. That number will decrease by one this morning as Starbucks unceremoniously shoves another family-owned coffee shop proudly serving commuters, college students and stroller-wielding moms since 1978, into bankruptcy and extinction.

"Here's the best part," she said while describing the responsibilities of a DoorDash employee. "I don't have to have any contact with the people who placed the order. I just drop it outside, take a picture with my phone letting them know I've delivered it, and then I leave!"

"That's like playing 'Ding Dong Ditch' with somebody's food," I said, referring to the game I played in my youth when bands of kids would ring somebody's doorbell and run away before the soon-to-be-annoyed homeowner answered. Looking back, I don't quite understand the concept. Why engage in mischief such as this if you can't even see the homeowner's outraged face?

Then again, when I played Ding Dong Ditch, homeowners were unlikely to answer their doors brandishing AR-15s loaded with full ammunition magazines. Ever wonder why you no longer see Christmas carolers come holiday time?

In 2023, according to a blog article posted by TeamStage, creators of a team management app, 36 percent of the American workforce, comprised of 57.3 million individuals, worked in the gig economy. Thirty-eight percent of these workers were between 18 and 34 while only 11 percent were over 55. So, while I am in the minority of gig workers age wise, I am in the majority because I am male. Thirty-one percent of men engage in gig work while only 18 percent of women elect to photograph a Starbucks Grande Latte they have just placed on somebody's back porch.

Surprisingly, creating their own schedules and making extra income were not the most popular reasons for gig work; rather it was the satisfaction of having more than one employer.

As a full-time comedian and public speaker, I have always had multiple employers. So the idea of adding one more didn't faze me. Besides, come end of year holiday time, my business slows down. I had the time. I just needed some incentive to get up every day.

I found the Amazon job on one of those employment websites but, come October, you can probably find Amazon "help wanted" job postings on the backs of cereal boxes. If hired, I would be "sorting, scanning and stacking packages on pallets, helping to get customer orders ready for delivery." The job paid $18 an hour and, shoes notwithstanding, offered no benefits unless I chose to make package stacking a career. Was my goal to spend my sexagenarian years working in a drafty warehouse and taking orders from the likes of Chad, one of my "supervisors?" This was a guy in his mid-20s, obligatory knit cap covering only a portion of his shoulder length hair who, after seeing me shrink wrap a full pallet of boxes that was not to his liking, told me I was "not in trouble" for doing it incorrectly.

"Thanks bro," I replied, trying to speak in Chad's vernacular although I wondered how I would handle being punished by a guy who smelled mildly of weed and wore a yellow vest, symbolizing his superiority over myself and my orange vest. More about color ranking later.

No, I am here because it is my long-term goal to learn enough about the inner workings of Amazon so I can approach their HR department and offer to do, unbeknownst to everybody on the warehouse floor, what I do best: Make them laugh about Amazon. I envisioned a full-time career at the company, traveling from sortation center to sortation center, giving 60-minute lectures on how to find joy and humor in a job that involved scanning bar codes eight hours a day while freezing or broiling your ass off because well, you work in a warehouse and make 18 bucks an hour.

I hoped to find a company that would offer me a work-from-home position but, like most organizations post-COVID, executives quickly realized their employees were more productive on site - as opposed to working from the comforts of their apartments dressed in pajamas and nuzzling their Golden Retrievers which required daily, four-hour walks. Therefore, I decided to apply for onsite positions and, once familiar with the company and its needs, snoop around for remote possibilities. Why not start with an organization that grosses $500 billion annually and employs over one million people, most of whom are currently scanning packages bound for Paris, Texas but that will most likely end up in Paris, France?

My spirits rose when upon showing up for my pre-hire interview at Amazon, an associate informed me the company promotes heavily from within its ranks and once I obtained 30 days of continuous employment, I could apply for jobs not visible to outside candidates. Thirty days sounded doable although I was a bit concerned about a sortation center associate's responsibilities, which included but were not limited to the ability to "stand, walk, push, pull, squat, bend and reach during shifts."

I was already paying enough in legal bills. Now it appeared my physical therapist would start cashing hefty checks if I didn't squat correctly.

My enthusiasm for a remote job, or any Amazon job for that matter, waned considerably when weeks after receiving my "Congratulations, you're hired!" email, I logged onto a national news publication's website and saw the headline "Amazon to lay off 10,000 workers!" The timing was baffling; Amazon was ramping up for the holiday season. Still, I thought, there MUST be a place for a 60-year-old comedian within Amazon's ranks. I would make my mark quickly by being the best and funniest, squatter on the floor. Maybe someday I could have Chad's job!

I barely got past the initial interview. I showed up on a warm November Saturday dressed, by Amazon standards, like I was heading to the opera. I wore a button-down oxford shirt and khakis, a far cry from other candidates headed into the hiring room. Most, by my observations, defined proper interview attire as "jeans with only a few holes" and baseball caps proclaiming allegiance to either a truck manufacturer or TRUMP.

I answered all the pre-hire questions flawlessly and was then instructed to enter a separate room for my drug test. Here is where the problems arose and by that, I don't mean I suddenly realized I should have snuck somebody else's urine into my khakis. A pleasant (at first anyway) woman instructed me to place a cotton swab in the side of my mouth and hold it there for approximately 10 minutes while saliva collected and the stick's exterior turned blue. For some reason, this task proved overwhelming and confusing to me. Hold it under my tongue? Against my cheek? Should I swallow? Would doing so produce saliva or rinse away the results? After 10 minutes, no blue was visible. I assumed that meant I was drug free. "Not so" the woman responded, opening another test kit and placing the swab in my mouth herself. She then retreated to a laptop computer and began typing. I assume she wrote "Candidate can't even put a swab in his mouth correctly. There is no way he has ever sucked a bong in his life."

An erroneous assumption on her part.

Eventually the stick turned blue enough, satisfying the proctor and allowing me to leave the facility embarrassed. Yet, five days later there it was: my official hiring email. I was now free to purchase shoes.

Three weeks later, Amazon photo ID in hand, I was strolling through the Amazon fulfillment center turnstiles past a sign proclaiming "Work hard, have fun, make history." I would quickly disagree with the last two components of that sentence, but it was my first day and I was hopeful. I was an "Amazonian," the title bestowed upon Amazon employees. What is it about tech companies that feel compelled to name their workers as if they were animal species? Spend a few hours in Silicon Valley and you will find yourself surrounded by "Googlers" (Google), "Pinployees" (Pinterest) and "Meta Mates" (the company formerly known as Facebook). Again, this annoying ID system seems to occur only in the tech world. I've never met a "Wal-Martian."

Day one consisted of meeting my future co-workers, in this case three women of various races and backgrounds. All three had previous Amazon holiday experience. Two had full time jobs outside of Amazon and, I assumed, were just looking to pick up extra money during the holiday season. The third entertained us with stories about horrible goings-on that occurred during her last go round with Amazon, including an active shooter incident. Yet here she was, back and eager to reenter the environment, albeit one hopefully void of a crazed sorter with a semi-automatic weapon.

When I mentioned I was a stand-up comedian, Chris, the employee tasked with familiarizing us with the warehouse, didn't even bat an eye. Instead, he informed us that people of various backgrounds and occupations also worked at Amazon.

"You'll see doctors and dentists on the floor," Chris proclaimed proudly. I made it my goal to converse with as many Amazonians as possible until I found one with a medical degree. Maybe he could look at my "squatting" technique and offer suggestions.

The tour began. We learned how to "clock in," a task I have never had to perform despite almost 40 years in the workforce. Then again, I've never had jobs centering around a timed shift. After graduating college with a journalism degree, I worked five years as a newspaper, and later as a television news reporter. Journalists don't clock in; we just show up. We work strange hours, drink when we aren't working and are paid solely for how much mayhem we share with subscribers or viewers. We collect overtime for covering murders on Christmas Day. Freelance journalists are often paid by the word, which is why Christmas Day murder stories include lines like "Upon arrival, police examined the area under the Christmas tree and found the victim very very very deceased."

After mastering the time clock, Chris showed us a vending machine containing not snacks, but Amazon attire and tools necessary to look and act the part of a sortation center warehouse employee. Behind the glass I saw box cutters, gloves and various colored vests, all free of charge. Chris selected orange-colored vests for myself and the other new hires. We donned them immediately; orange identified us as new workers as we headed onto the warehouse floor. It also identified us as workers so clueless about the sorting process that we were bound to eventually get run over by a forklift before our shifts ended. Upon donning the vest, I felt better knowing that if my Amazon employment didn't work out, a second career as a school crossing guard was within my grasp, for I was already properly attired.

From there we took a quick tour of the massive sorting warehouse, taking care to stay within the green taped lines that designated we were (hopefully) safe from a runaway forklift but not an active shooter. I was baffled for I saw very few forklifts, or activity of any sort, as we continued the tour. A few employees with scanners here, a guy moving a pallet there, but not the frenzy one would expect a week before the official start of the holiday shopping season known as Black Friday.

Gazing upward, however, I saw a different story writing itself. The Crest Hill facility was capable of processing over 1 million packages per day and that goal certainly looked obtainable. Box after box after box zipped along conveyor belts at lighting speeds, their destinations unknown to me but most likely bound for my front porch, thanks to my wife's zeal for Amazon. Say one thing about Amazon; any ordered item can be placed in a box. How many times have you ordered tiny items such as micro storage disks for your computer, only to find them on your front porch encased in a cardboard carton that could easily double as a "fort" for a child and his friends?

Tubes, ramps and funnels (most painted in bright yellow) comprised the warehouse's interior. The whole thing reminded me of an indoor waterpark but one void of hyperactive children, obese adults in bathing suits, overpriced corn dogs or fun.

After showing us the various workstations around the warehouse and promising we would eventually be working at most of them, Chris led us to a classroom facility near the entrance where we would spend the next four hours learning about Amazon "culture." Our education consisted of watching various videos featuring poorly animated Amazon workers of different races and head wear. Hijabs and burkas were popular among female animated Amazonians.

Occasionally, a pop quiz followed featuring ridiculous questions and even more ridiculous multiple-choice answers:

"Sarah is on her way to her station in the warehouse when a male co-worker tells her she looks "SMOKIN' HOT IN THOSE STEEL-TOED SHOES!" Should Sarah…

A) Kick him in the groin
B) Order another, less attractive pair of shoes from Zappos
C) Ask to be reassigned to a department where bare feet are considered acceptable
D) None of the above but open to discussion

Before we even had a chance to answer, the instructor hovered the mouse over the correct answer, in this case 'D," and answered for us. This went on for the better part of two hours.

We learned Amazon lingo and the definition of a "falling object" which is "An object that falls from one height to another." We were told that, if we see an object that we determine is "falling," the best solution is "don't try to catch it." My mind raced back to those millions of boxes I saw whizzing over my head and wondering why the Amazon vending machine didn't include hard hats.

An HR specialist taught us the "Five S's: Sort, Straighten, Shine, Standardize, Sustain." I added a sixth, muttering "Shit" under my breath. We learned how to apply for extra shifts, the trouble we'd find ourselves in if we clocked in too late or, much to my surprise, too EARLY. I always thought showing up 15 minutes prior to anything, save maybe a dinner party or an outing with your in-laws, meant you were punctual and responsible. At Amazon, it meant you just wreaked havoc in the payroll department.

We learned about daily contests that could yield prizes such as (SURPRISE) Amazon gift cards if we emerged victorious. We learned how to master the "five-star stance." It did not cover the proper way to squat but it did caution against slouching and the health hazards of looking down at one's phone too much. It should be noted that the instructor for this session was John, an employee who I pegged to be about twelve. It should also be noted that after pressing 'play' on the video, John spent the next four minutes slouched at his desk scrolling through his phone.

The sun was setting when I exited the sortation center, a full week before I would begin my first day. I felt confident, even if my Zappos bowling shoes were killing me.

We reconvened the following Friday, coincidentally Black Friday itself. To me that seemed like the absolute worst day to be training new Amazonians. I offered to return in mid-January, but Chris said that shockingly, the warehouse wasn't that busy today and it would be a great day for training. Skeptical, we followed him like ducklings behind their mother into the cavernous facility. We clocked in and selected gloves and harnesses from the vending machine. The harness, Chris explained, would be worn over our vests and would hold our scanners, the primary tool of a sortation center worker. Figuring out how to wear a harness, incidentally, is like untangling Christmas lights. On my second day, I had to google "How to put on an Amazon harness for scanning." Had I not done this, I would have clocked in at least 30 minutes late.

We first used the scanners to scan our ID badges. An on-screen message then directed every scanned employee to the warehouse location where their shift would commence. "Break room" was not a choice.

Because it was our first day, no assignments appeared so Chris motioned us to follow him to the warehouse's rear, where we would be assigned to specific sortation areas. Upon receiving my scanner, I noticed the name "Zebra Technologies" on the exterior and remembered that I had performed stand-up comedy for that very company in the late 1990s. I chose to keep that information to myself unless I met a doctor or dentist. THEY would be impressed.

Chris demonstrated how to get the scanner up and running by pushing "Sort Center/Build Container/Trickle" on the touch screen. To this day, I have no idea what trickle means or if I ever trickled correctly during my time at Amazon.

Amazon has not only redefined retail shopping but also the English language, as evidenced by the assortment of signs and white boards that hung throughout the warehouse. One conveyor belt, labeled "K3," contained a pink sign underneath proclaiming:

HOU5
DAY CPT
13:00

And an orange sign under that labeled:

HCH2
CYC 2
SUN CPT
07:00

I do know K3 was the name of the actual station, meaning a supervisor could come up to me any time and say "they need some help on K3." As for the rest of the gibberish, I have no idea.

Ditto for the white board featuring instructions or commands (I still don't know which but I'm sure weed-smoking Chad does) in multicolored Sharpie ink such as:

DAY TWO
Sortation
1) Container Build ⇒ KITL *
2) Splitter/Facer/Pickoff ⇒ KITL *
3) Dangerous Good Module ⇒ in preferred language

Not to be confused with:

INBOUND

1) Inbound Fluid Unload ⇒ KITL *
2) Inbound Safety School ⇒ in preferred language

OTHER

Containerization

3) GoCart Combined training ⇒ KIT*

READ LABELS

- Cross-Dock XD
- Old label sideload/dump
- MDWS waterspider/PSA

In between all the acronyms, terms like "water spider," "shuttle dump," "jam clear," "prism" and "gatekeeper" were written around the warehouse. None of these terms were covered in the previous week's videos.

The other employees and I stood at the base of a conveyor belt, our eyes gazing up at a chute where Amazon boxes of various sizes and quantities would eventually appear, slide (or in some cases violently tumble) down a ramp and come to a screeching halt. We took over from there. It was my job to locate the proper bar code on the box, and trust me there were several to choose from, and then locate the pallet with the identical code. The process went like this: Remove the box from the belt, place it on the pallet, scan the box's barcode and scan the pallet's code. A high pitched "beep" meant the tasks were done correctly and in the correct order. A low sounding beep meant I had screwed up and I might be "in trouble."

We also received small "scanner error" cards containing scenarios of why we kept hearing low pitched beeps and what to do should that occur. For example, if my scanner said "Package 2 not scanned to the container. Scan both packages to the container" then I was supposed to "Scan a different package on the pallet. Then go back and scan the first package you tried to scan to the container. DO NOT hit 'refresh.'"

Or I could just toss the incorrectly scanned package onto an incorrectly labeled pallet, hit 'refresh' and continue working. Sorry three-year-old in Santa Fe who received a case of wine three days before Christmas. Also, sorry to the foodie in Minneapolis who received the LeapFrog Rainbow Learning Lights Mixer. My bad.

If I received "Wrong building. This container is missorted and not intended for this building" then "The package was intended for a different Sorting Center. Press 'refresh' and place the package on the Problem Solving pallet."

Or I could just toss the incorrectly scanned package onto an incorrectly labeled pallet and…well you get the idea. Sorry, 83-year-old woman in Sunrise, Florida who received a Super Mario Gaming Chair. Further apologies to the 11-year-old boy in Bismarck, North Dakota who spent Christmas morning playing with a wireless hand massager that can provide temporary relief from arthritis and Carpal Tunnel Syndrome. My bad again.

Stacking the boxes was akin to playing Tetris, the online game where different colored shapes drop from the top of a computer screen and the player must quickly manipulate them into perfect horizontal rows without empty space. Some of the more seasoned sortation center employees knew exactly how to accomplish this. I marveled at their ability to take skinny, rectangular boxes that looked like they housed long-range rifles, and somehow jam them into an array of square boxes that I had meticulously assembled.

Eventually the pallet grew to about eight feet in height, signaling it was time to shrink wrap the entire monstrosity and, hopefully, not incur Chad's wrath. Once completed, another Amazon employee came by with a pallet jack and moved it to God knows where. An empty pallet appeared in the space and we started the process all over again.

If there is a more boring job than Amazon sortation center employee, I'd like to know what it is. My shifts were between four and six hours, some beginning at 5 p.m. After about 15 minutes of scanning, stacking and shrink wrapping, I began looking at my watch or my phone, wondering what the hell I was doing in a warehouse surrounded by co-workers who looked as if they'd been in prison as recently as the previous morning. Amazon sortation center employees are not paid by how many boxes they scan, only how many hours they work. Therefore, I found myself drifting away from my position and aimlessly walking through the warehouse, attempting to look important but, in reality, avoiding my duties. I'm sure my ruse convinced nobody; after all, I was wearing an orange vest.

"It's a learning experience," I kept telling myself. "When you are lecturing these workers about having fun at work and how easy it can be to laugh while scanning, you'll be able to draw from personal experience!"

After two weeks of this tedium, I decided I was done. My back and foot pain had intensified, and I still had not mastered the art of correctly stacking a pallet, or shrink wrapping its contents. Even though I was halfway to the magical 30-day number, I was convinced nobody on the Amazon floor, regardless of vest color, was interested in my dream of becoming the funniest Amazon trainer this side of Jeff Bezos' yacht. Whenever I approached senior Amazon workers – aka workers who had graduated beyond wearing vests of any color – with my training idea, they half listened while eyeing me suspiciously. Who was this guy in an orange vest attempting to change the culture at Amazon? Through humor? I would have been more believable if I approached a worker severely injured from a forklift incident, and said, "Don't worry. I'm a doctor."

I found the pop-up HR department on the warehouse floor, explained my dilemma and resigned. The last time I did that was 1989 when I told my bosses at WPTV in West Palm Beach, Florida that I was quitting broadcast journalism to pursue my dream as a stand-up comedian. This time around, my only dream was to find gig work where I could sit.

It didn't take long.

"Too bad that all the people who know how to run this country are busy driving taxicabs and cutting hair."

– ***Attributed to George Burns*** (BrainyMedia 2024)

I) Side Hustle #2 – You Will Not Puke in my Vehicle!

Today I picked up two girls at the local high school. Wait, it's not what you think. Please keep reading and do not forward this book to your local law enforcement authorities. For I am not a creep, a pervert or a bad person, despite what my ex-wife may have told her attorney.

I am an Uber driver.

That's right, I didn't get arrested for that high school trip; instead I earned $8.22 for it. It could have been more but, as I discovered, high school girls don't understand the concept of tipping. Strange, because the "would you care to leave a tip?" prompt appears on a passenger's phone mere seconds after exiting an Uber driver's vehicle. And since these girls never stopped staring at their phones, even DURING the exit process, they had ample chance to pad my bank account.

Uber was founded in 2009 by Garrett Camp and Travis Kalanick, two San Francisco tech bros who, I assume, finally tired of walking up hills in their home city. I don't blame them. By nature, I am a huge explorer of new destinations via foot. It's not unusual for me to walk down a strange alleyway in an unfamiliar city and, two hours later, have clocked more than 20,000 steps on my

Apple Watch. Thankfully, none were obtained running from would be muggers but I'm sure that day is coming.

San Francisco, on the other hand, will eventually force even the most ardent walkers to call it quits and find a vehicle, ANY vehicle, to complete their journeys. Brinks trucks have been stolen in San Francisco, not because their contents contain hundreds of thousands of dollars, but because burglars planning to walk to and from homes they hoped to ransack simply couldn't handle the inclines. I am not familiar enough with San Francisco to provide directions, but I have enough experience to confidently tell any confused tourist that their destination is at the top of a steep hill. Except for Alcatraz, which is on an island in a bay that spills into an ocean. Even Uber can't get you there.

Camp and Kalanick solved their walking dilemma with an idea that violates every rule elementary school children learn in a "Stranger Danger" assembly. If you're an Uber passenger, it's now perfectly acceptable to get into a stranger's car. If you're an Uber driver, it's fine and dandy to allow strangers to enter your vehicle. During COVID, Uber added one rule: Those strangers had to be wearing masks. Otherwise, anything goes.

I should point out that the idea of using personal vehicles to transport passengers was not invented by either Camp or Kalanick. In the mid- '90s, with the internet in its infancy and the word "app" foreign to everyone, particularly those of us still trying to figure out how to correctly copy and paste, I found myself in New York City. Business nearly completed, I called a car service 24 hours in advance to arrange a ride from the Javits Center to LaGuardia. The next day, luggage in hand, I stood on 11th Avenue watching multiple town cars whiz by but none slowing down to pick up a guy with luggage and a flight departure growing closer. When I called the service, a, judging by his accent, lifelong New Yorker said, "Yeah, traffic is backed up on the bridge."

He said this as if I should have known what "bridge" he was referring to and planned accordingly. Like, instead of making the reservation for 4 p.m., I should have suggested 10:30 a.m.

"You do realize I have a flight to catch?" I asked.

"You want the car, or don't you?" came the reply.

Eventually a silver Toyota Tercel pulled up. A driver speaking in broken English with a strong Russian accent said he would "gets" me to LaGuardia immediately, for a price far less than the car service. I quickly agreed and off we went. He was correct in his assertion that the ride would be quicker, mostly because he took a series of short cuts that involved driving through school playgrounds and back yards whenever possible. But make no mistake, he "gots" me there.

Despite this ludicrous and perilous way of earning income, the ride share phenomenon intrigued me, even before my divorce. I first heard of Uber via a friend, a well-known Washington DC TV anchorman. Upon exiting a restaurant and after a few glasses of wine, he whipped out his phone and, while tapping a few commands, told me his station bosses suggested he "Uber" home whenever he'd consumed alcohol. Before I even had the chance to ask him what the hell he was talking about, an unmarked black SUV pulled over to the curb where we were standing. My friend wished me well, got in and sped away. I was left wondering if I had just witnessed a local celebrity's kidnapping and if I would ever see him alive again.

A few months later, while speaking in San Diego, curiosity got the best of me and I ordered my first Uber. I typed in my destination and then stared at my Uber app as an automobile emoji moved continually closer to the red dot that I assumed represented me. Watching the emoji navigate roads made me want to hit "cancel" multiple times. Whoever was driving looked like he had stolen his parent's automobile for the weekend and was showing off his driving "skills" to his friends in the backseat. It fishtailed numerous times as it rounded curves, reversed while in motion and, at one point, looked as if it had entered a body of water yet did not sink. It just kept moving, eventually getting back on dry land and continuing its journey. I became excited at the thought that James Bond might be picking me up.

Once my driver, a twenty something dude who for all I know could have been Camp or Kalanick, arrived, I climbed into the back seat and said nothing until we arrived at my destination approximately 12 minutes later. From there I remained in the back seat, unsure what to do next.

"Is this the right place?" my driver eventually asked.

"Uh yeah, I think so," I replied. "Do we settle up now?"

"No, you just get out," he said upon realizing that his Uber passenger had no idea what Uber was. And I'll admit, after years of arguing with cab drivers who insisted they only accept cash despite the CREDIT CARD reader mounted to the plexiglass separating us, I was flummoxed that no money changed hands. I exited the vehicle, convinced I had somehow scammed my driver. My credit card statement showed otherwise.

I spent the next few years taking numerous Ubers and its chief competitor, Lyft, to destinations around the country and around the world. Like all riders, I've had my share of unique drivers. There was the guy who showed up barefoot, forcing me to google "Is it legal to drive barefoot in Illinois?" as we sped toward Midway Airport. It is.

There was the female driver who, upon opening her trunk so I could hoist my luggage inside, had to move a set of sheets and two pillows, leading me to wonder if her vehicle was also her home. There was another female driver who asked if I could ride in the front seat because her "associate," a toddler in a car seat, was strapped in the back. While en route to the airport, she told me she had recently lost her job as a home healthcare worker and ride sharing was for the time being, her sole source of income. Her story overwhelmed me so that I tipped her $100 cash upon exiting. I still remember the tears welling in her eyes.

There was the stocky, crew cutted man who, when I asked if he had another job, looked menacingly at me in the rear-view mirror and growled "Sir, I would prefer to keep details of my secondary occupation confidential." His response led me to glance at the back seat door handles and wonder how badly I would be injured if I leapt from a moving vehicle? Harrison Ford has done it numerous times in Indiana Jones movies and he always manages to dust himself off and continue his quest for whatever treasure he is chasing. Luckily, we arrived at my destination before I had to replicate Jones' moves.

And then there was the kid, 19 at most, who picked up myself and two co-workers in the midst of a video shoot in Long Island, New York. We had just learned our return flight to Chicago had been cancelled and we would be forced to spend another night in the Big Apple. After securing reservations, we were headed to Queens for dinner bemoaning our situation loudly in the back seat. As the ride continued our driver entered the conversation with the most unlikely of propositions:

"Guys, say the word and I will drive you to Chicago right now."

A distance of 790 miles.

I looked at the driver's eyes in the rear-view mirror searching for a sign that he was joking. He wasn't. He was ready; we just had to agree on a price.

Speaking for the group, I declined the offer but complimented him on his entrepreneurial spirit. If Uber ever launches a long-distance app called "Uber, No I'm Totally Serious," I will immediately think of this driver and assume he had something to do with it.

Because I enjoy talking to strangers and hearing their stories, my conversations with Uber drivers usually centered around this compelling side hustle. Why were they driving for Uber I asked. Did they make decent money? Was it their full-time job? How much time did they spend behind the wheel per day? Per week? Per month?

The more information I obtained, the more I thought rideshare driving might be far more fun and productive, than stacking Amazon packages. This, despite the potential dangers of entering strange neighborhoods, housing developments, industrial parks and apartment complexes to pick up people who, before the creation of rideshare would have been labeled "hitchhikers" as opposed to "passengers." So in December 2022, I clicked "sign up to drive" on the Uber website and began the qualification process.

If you're not currently incarcerated, you are qualified to drive for Uber. Don't speak English? No worries. There's no grammar test involved. True, there is a background check but basically you take a picture of your driver's license, your vehicle registration and insurance cards, upload them to the Uber app…and then wait. While you're waiting, Uber requires you take a "rules of the road" test featuring questions that start easy and got even more simple as the test progresses. Amazon culture questions were more difficult. I half expected the final question to be "True or False? In Illinois it is illegal to operate a moving vehicle with one hand while mixing a vodka martini with the other."

Brief videos covered subjects like what to do if a passenger hits on me sexually, passes out drunk in the back seat or announces he or she was going to be sick. I vowed to eliminate the last two situations by never driving at night and never picking up passengers at bars, although I'm sure drunks tip better than high school cheerleaders. Regarding the unwanted sexual advances, I elected to adopt a "wait and see" approach. Hey, who hasn't gotten horny at 7 a.m.?

After a few days of checking the app and being told my background check was still "in process," I received the congratulatory email stating that yes, I was officially an Uber driver. I downloaded and printed the Uber logo and slapped it on my front passenger windshield. I completed my profile, which would be visible to any Uber passenger to read while waiting for me to arrive. It looked like this:

Fun fact: I drive for Uber because I'm a full-time stand-up comedian and I find people fascinating. If you want to talk and laugh during our ride, great! Otherwise, I'll shut up and get you where you need to go. Welcome aboard!

Other experience: Stand-up comedian and newspaper humor columnist

Why I drive: I like to hear other people's stories. Everybody has one. What's yours?

Profile completed, I purchased one of those cell phone car mounts so I could accept rides while (mostly) keeping my eyes on the road. Then I connected my iPhone, opened the app and waited for my first fare.

It didn't take long. A chime, accompanied by a screen showing the address and the $10.14 I would make for this ride, appeared. I was to pick up Darlene at a residential address and deliver her to what I later learned was a medical facility 10.3 miles away. When I arrived, I waited beyond the 90 seconds Uber allows passengers to get their shit together and enter the vehicle. After that, the clock starts and they are charged a late fee. An elderly woman appeared shortly thereafter, oblivious to the fact that I had just pocketed an extra NINE CENTS for her tardiness.

Darlene informed me that yes, she was on her way to a doctor's office for a heart test. You see, Darlene had heart disease, no she had cataracts, no she had an artificial hip, wait she also had bad knees. All her maladies spilled from her mouth during the ride. We also had time to discuss our favorite cruise lines and destinations. She arrived safe and in one piece, although Darlene seemed to be in multiple pieces judging by her medical history.

Shortly after dropping her off, I received a message stating Darlene had tipped me five bucks. This Uber thing could be fun I thought, providing gas prices continued to decline. Luckily, I did not decide to drive for Uber in Summer 2022 when a gallon of gas cost more than a glass of French Beaujolai. My daughter's DoorDash career occurred during this time. I once asked if she was actually making any money after paying fuel expenses. She declined to comment; remember, she enjoyed DoorDashing because she didn't have to engage in conversation.

My first day continued delightfully. My fares included a restaurant owner from my hometown who wanted to talk golf as we headed to his business; a man dropping off his own vehicle for service and in need of a ride back to his house. He worked in the nuclear power industry but my job as a stand-up comedian still trumped his profession and he was only too happy to hear about how I got started in the business, once I admitted that's what I did for a living. It was then I realized Uber could be more than a way to pad my bank account, curtail loneliness and maybe provide some laughs; it could also serve as a chance to obtain work in my primary profession. I have always liberally dropped the "I'm a full-time stand-up comedian" line into casual conversation, simply because it intrigues people. If your Uber driver tells you he or she is a full-time insurance sales rep, you will most likely spend the rest of your ride scrolling through TikTok videos. But hearing "comedian" leads to curiosity. I made it my mission, then and there, to always try and ask my riders what they did for a living, simply so I could reciprocate and tell them what I did. That's networking at its most basic.

The day ended when I picked up a family of four headed to O'Hare for a Thanksgiving getaway in Las Vegas. Mom and Dad had two daughters who looked to be about ten and seven. Nobody cared that I was a stand-up comedian, nor did they respond when I reminded the girls to always split aces and always stand when the dealer is showing a six.

My second day was just as pleasant. It began at 4:20 a.m. when I picked up a UPS employee on his way to work. True, picking up strange people in strange locations in total darkness has its challenges but eventually I found him. Upon entering the vehicle, he immediately asked me if I had satellite radio as he wanted to listen to some soccer match taking place on the other side of the globe. My answer disappointed him but he tipped me anyway.

At first, driving for Uber is nothing short of addicting and a huge ego boost. Think about it, you turn on your phone and wait for people to request…YOU! OK, maybe not you personally; I never had a passenger enter my vehicle and say "I have been standing here, waiting for a soon to be divorced corporate comedian to swing by. And here you are!"

But when a passenger requests an Uber, and I accept, I've inserted myself into that rider's life. Passengers count on ME to keep their lives running smoothly. And dropping off a passenger, only to realize another passenger was waiting close by with the same needs, was enticing. Unfortunately, it also led to a few uncomfortable moments when I found myself in less than desirable neighborhoods. Uber, incidentally, does charge higher rates for riders in these 'hoods but the app doesn't tell me, the driver, that I'm about to enter "turf." Some local neighborhood knowledge is always a good idea before deciding to drive for Uber. One afternoon, while driving in Oak Park, Illinois, a Chicago suburb containing both multimillionaires and street gangs, a couple entered my Lincoln reeking of weed. Luckily, they weren't going too far. I dropped them off and accepted another ride, soon finding myself at a hospital to pick up an elderly gentleman who had just completed an outpatient procedure.

As we drove away, I asked the obvious.

"Does my car reek of weed?"

"I wasn't going to say anything…but yes," he responded.

"It's not me."

"I believe you," he said. We spent the rest of the ride discussing college football. After dropping him off, I paused requests, long enough to find a drugstore where I purchased an industrial sized can of air freshener.

Looking at my profile page eleven months later, I had completed 464 Uber trips. I had obtained a 4.98 rating out of 5. I had been complimented for "excellent service" and having a "neat and tidy" vehicle. Obviously, the air freshener did its job.

Of those who bothered to rate me, 246 gave me five-star reviews. One passenger gave me one star and I would sure as hell like that passenger to step forward and explain why. You're in MY car, taking advantage of MY fuel and MY car payments. Unless I drive you over a cliff, I should get five stars.

Three weeks after signing up, I had netted approximately $1000 yet received only $80 in gratuities. Two words about tipping your rideshare driver: DO IT! First for the reasons I just laid out. You are entering a space that, in my case anyway, is clean, comfortable and safe. You pressed a button on your phone and a vehicle magically appeared. And before you grumble that the trip to the airport is costing you $65 and you don't think I'm worth that amount, remember that Uber drivers net approximately 40 percent of fares. Shocking, sad and true. Camp, Kalanick and their cronies at Uber take the rest.

Financial reasons aside, there's a mental high that accompanies receiving a gratuity. I can't explain it but it exists. Believe me when I say that, if Jeff Bezos, Warren Buffett and Bill Gates drove Uber for a day, they would still compare tips at day's end. Like me, they would be annoyed when extra services went unnoticed. I have multiple stories I could share with the trio. There was the woman I picked up at Walmart carrying more than a dozen grocery bags, which I loaded into my trunk and then carried to her apartment's front door.

No tip.

There was another woman, waiting for me outside a motel accompanied by a car seat containing a sleeping infant. Reeking of weed, "mom" placed the seat next to her not bothering to use a seat belt to secure her child. Even though it had been 25 years since I threaded a safety belt through a car seat, I did it for her. After a 45-minute ride there was neither a tip nor a "thank you."

Mind you, I am not demanding every passenger add 15, 20, 25 percent or a custom amount of their choice. I don't know every passenger's situation. I drove several passengers who I picked up at their places of employment and dropped them at their NEXT place of employment. If you are working multiple jobs to make ends meet, please keep your money. It's my pleasure to offer door-to-door service.

However, if you are on your way to San Francisco for a company function and brought your spouse because you "plan to spend a few extra days in the Bay Area," you are not suffering financially; at least, not immediately. Oh, and that bag I lifted in and out of my trunk? What the hell was in it? Perhaps you're saving my tip money for the amount the airline will charge you once you put your suitcase on that scale. Pony up!

Six months after beginning my Uber career, I moved from my quaint Chicago suburb to the city itself, placing my Lincoln in a potential customer pool that had just increased by approximately 2.95 million passengers. The traffic I encountered backed up that number. I contemplated whether to continue driving for Uber, find another side hustle or abandon my car completely and just rely on busses, subways, my trusty bicycle, or other Uber drivers to get me where I needed to go. I elected to keep the car and my Uber status but grumbled while filling my tank at stations charging 20 cents more per gallon of gas than I was paying in the 'burbs. Then there's the red-light cameras that apparently have been placed at every Chicago intersection, or at least the ones I apparently failed to stop at. Envelopes from the City of Chicago regularly appeared in my mailbox, containing visual proof of my Lincoln's existence on streets where the speed limit was lower than what I thought it should be. I racked up $700 in fines, not exactly a great return on my investment in gig work.

If you feel the human race is bound for extinction due to the fact that we don't care about global warming, Middle East crises or the January 6th insurrection, I encourage you to drive for Uber and strike up conversations with passengers, for you will quickly learn about their hopes, their dreams, their personal situations – both good and bad – and their willingness to share all of it with a stranger.

The pandemic, and the ensuing isolation, shut us down from face-to-face communication. Despite those who claimed to embrace this new way of life and vowed they would NEVER return to the office where they HAVE to TALK with other HUMANS, I do believe society missed communicating with one another and we are making up for lost time. While I cannot remember all 464 occupants who shared my Lincoln – hell I'm 61 and can barely remember where I left my laptop containing this book's contents - I wish to thank a select few who I found so entertaining, or just interesting. It was free therapy for a guy navigating a traumatic life change.

I tended to drive for Uber on weekend mornings, when traffic was at its lightest yet there were still plenty of residents and visitors who needed to get somewhere. One September Sunday morning, after completing an O'Hare run and heading back into the city, I found myself near the DePaul University campus when my phone chimed. Rose was requesting a ride. I arrived at the location, in this case a street corner as opposed to a personal residence, and saw four girls all in their early 20s and all wearing short black cocktail dresses, approaching. As they got closer, I realized Rose was among them and I would be picking up four fares, not one.

They piled into my vehicle; it should be noted that my Lincoln Nautilus qualified for Uber "Comfort" status because it was an SUV and, comparatively, a more expensive vehicle than the heaps of twisted metal and plastic driven by most Uber drivers. But it was also capable of holding four passengers, tops. Rose and her group qualified, but barely.

Three folded themselves into the back seat with Rose riding shotgun next to me. They all reeked of vodka and clearly had been partying all night. I had spent the same Saturday evening retrieving dust bunnies from beneath my refrigerator, so I was more than eager to hear how Rose and her compatriots had spent theirs. In a span of a few minutes, I learned the following:

Their night began on a rooftop bar, at a party hosted by someone whose name they couldn't recall.

Somehow, they found themselves in "the hood" but none could remember how, or why, they ended up there.

Luckily "Victor" rescued them from the hood although they don't like Victor because he has this annoying habit of watching other people have sex and then finishing on his own. It took about three minutes to glean that nugget of information.

"Victor is such a cock sometimes!" I heard from the backseat.

I silently prayed I would never pick up Victor.

After leaving the 'hood, the girls ended up naked in a hot tub, although I didn't ask where. Somehow, they managed to get back into their clothes and call for me. Rather than dispute any component of their stories, I elected to probe them for more information. Hey, once a journalist, always a journalist. But just as I was about to inquire about their sexual habits – hey, once a male, always a male – the dad in me took over. These girls were about the ages of my daughters, and I hoped I have raised them not to be drunk, promiscuous or attracted to guys named Victor. At least not simultaneously. While I admired the group's sense of adventure, I couldn't help wondering if one would eventually be found dead in a trash heap if they continued their ways.

"You ladies are being safe, right?" I asked. "Staying together at all times?"

"Oh sure," Rose said, but I had my doubts.

"I assume you are all going home to bed now?" I asked.

"Oh NOOOOO!" one replied from the back seat. "We are going to change clothes and then head out to brunch. Then we'll do it all over again tonight."

Ahhh, youth.

Uber also has taught me to realize that, as dire as my situation seemed some days, others have it far worse. One wintry afternoon, I picked up Larry at a large apartment complex in the suburb adjoining mine. Larry had requested a "multiple stop" ride, meaning I would be taking him to one location and, in this case, waiting to drop him at the next location. Larry got in, noticed the two books I had previously authored and strategically placed in the passenger seat pocket in hopes they would lead to conversations, or even Amazon sales, and inquired about my job as a comedian.

We chatted amiably about comedy while I piloted him to his first location, a local liquor store.

"They know me in here and I know exactly what I want," he said. "I shouldn't be more than three minutes."

Two minutes and thirty-seven seconds later, he returned, a bottle of dark rum in hand. I know next to nothing about rum brands as I am, exclusively, a vodka and beer drinker, but I asked him about his choice. My second stop was a return to his apartment. He wished me luck in my career as he left my car. I turned off the app and thought nothing of the encounter.

Two months later, I was driving in the same area when a fare popped up. Turning into an apartment complex, I detected a note of familiarity. It was then I remembered picking up Larry "the liquor store guy" in this very complex.

Although Uber riders can use Google Maps, Waze or other navigational apps to locate rides, Uber has its own and, I have to admit, it's quite good. Kudos to Camp and Kalanick! Not only does it have immense knowledge of streets and expressways, but also back alleys.

Following the voice commands, I drove halfway around a large, circular parking lot and waited for my ride. Now the sense of déjà vu was in full swing as I realized this was precisely the unit where I picked up Larry. No way would…

As I attempted to complete that thought, Larry emerged. He didn't remember me at first.

"Didn't I pick you up a few months ago? I'm the comedian," I said.

"Oh yeah," he replied in the same friendly tone I recalled. "How's it going?"

"I took you to the liquor store, right?"

"And you're doing it again," he said.

The trip was identical; stop at liquor store, wait in parking lot, retrieve Larry and his bottle of rum. This time I was less chatty on the ride back to Larry's apartment for I realized this was most likely, a recurring, perhaps daily, event for him. I decided Larry was probably an alcoholic and was prohibited from driving due to multiple DUI arrests. None of that may be true but it was the story I elected to go with, for it made me realize there are people in the world with problems far worse than getting divorced after 29 years of marriage.

In between Rose and Larry, there were countless other fares: The truck driver who constantly referred to me as "Old School;" the 20-something girl whose profile requested a "quiet car" but wouldn't shut up about her job status and upcoming interview for the entire ride; the St. Louis dad, in Chicago for the weekend with his eight-year-old daughter for a youth gymnastics tournament, who kept peppering me with questions about my health insurance needs; the passengers, too numerous to mention, who began conversations with "I don't mean to bring up politics but…;" the couple who requested me after a previous friendly ride but, this time, announced their trip would include their two drugged-up dogs.

The kid who left an Airpod in my car; the guy who left his WALLET in my car; the nine months pregnant woman who was, rightfully, perturbed when I made a wrong turn. Every moment counts when you're expecting, I guess.

Overheard phone conversations while driving:

I just got my food stamps today…do you want me to cook tonight or should we go out?...Okay, get the two lobster tails out of the freezer. I'll make those.

Hi. I'm just checking on the status of the restraining order.

If he doesn't give a fuck, then I don't give two fucks.

It is SO hard to find a decent dog walker today.

Eighteen months after becoming an Uber driver, I deleted my app and removed myself from Uber's ranks. I'd made the decision to sell my car and, for the time being, join the thousands of Chicago residents whose worlds and credit card statements are free of gas charges, insurance premiums and repairs. I'd added 13,000 miles to my car's odometer and made about $10,000, if one doesn't count the red light camera ticket fees. But I realized a serious incident was in my future. City driving is fraught with dangers one doesn't find in the suburbs. Other vehicles darting out of alleys, cyclists constantly in your right blind spot because your car is traveling precariously close to their anointed bike lanes, and dogs on 50-foot leashes about to enter crosswalks while their clueless owners stare at their phones. Also, as one car-less passenger told me, "Seventy-five percent of Chicago residents don't carry car insurance so good luck if you have an accident."

He might be right. Somebody else can have the hassle of owning a 2019 Lincoln Nautilus. I plan to rely on my God-given legs and my trusty bicycle to get around my beloved city. Who knows? Maybe I'd find another "gig" opportunity using these tools.

It didn't take long.

"Get a bicycle. You will not regret it. If you live."

– *Mark Twain* (Twain 2019)

J) Side Hustle #3 – Crossing Michigan Avenue on Bikes. What Could Possibly Go Wrong?

In March 2023, I was sitting in a Richmond, Virginia-area Airbnb and, out of boredom, scrolling LinkedIn. Suddenly, a job post caught my eye:

WANTED: Chicago Tour Guides! Show off the city you love. Flexible schedule.

"Interesting" I thought, scrolling further to learn more about the organization CityExperiences.com. "I could see myself doing this. And it doesn't involve scanning packages or picking up strangers in my car."

Should I land an interview I thought, at least I could tell the HR department that I had previous tour guide experience, providing it's OK to bring up jobs I held 35 years ago. While a student at Northwestern University, I volunteered to lead prospective students and their parents in 45-minute tours around the campus. The parents spent most of the excursion with pained looks on their faces, their lips occasionally moving in silent prayer, asking a higher being to help their child reconsider and opt for a community college. Or at least a state school. Even in 1984, the price tag for a Northwestern education was among the highest in the country. I managed to cobble tuition together via a variety of financial aid programs and scholarships that required creativity when filling out the applications:

My philanthropic activities include holding a major position in my high school's "Just Say No to Drugs" campaign.

Technically that was true. Up until that point, nobody had ever offered me drugs.

As a campus guide, I spent most of the tour trying out comedy bits on the participants, as I was already immersed in what would eventually be my full-time profession. Not all the material was original, I will admit. One favorite joke, used by all the guides, was to talk about the student library built adjacent to the university's theatre building.

We began by telling our enraptured guests that the library was slowly sinking into Lake Michigan because architect Walter Netsch, when designing the structure, failed to consider the weight of books that would be housed there. It's an urban myth but was a perfect setup for the joke that followed. Turning our guests' attention to the theatre building, we said, "This building too is sinking into Lake Michigan. It seems engineers failed to consider the weight of the average theatre major's ego."

Ba Dump Bang!

Campus Tour Guide Giver also allowed me to brush up on my improvisational skills as I had to quickly answer questions ranging from the common – "Is it safe to walk this campus at night?" – to the inane.

"Where is the easiest location to buy drugs," one high school senior asked during the tour.

For the record, the answers to these two questions, in order, are "Yes, but it's best to walk in groups" and "These are you parents standing next to you, right?"

Now I felt ready to resurrect my tour guide skills while standing under Chicago's L tracks and shouting over the din of a city with a population of 3 million, as opposed to a 6,500-student enrollment.

I filled out the application. The next day Matt, a recruitment professional/content creator/creative problem solver according to his LinkedIn profile, contacted me. Matt invited me to pick an interview time on his virtual calendar. Two days later, via Zoom, Matt told me I was "exactly what we are looking for" and he would "be in touch."

The phrase "be in touch" never seems to end positively. Over the years I've learned, via potential clients and girlfriends, that "be in touch" is a polite way of eliminating future communication. Matt affirmed that by ghosting me. Follow up emails and LinkedIn messages netted silence. Maybe he got wind of the theatre joke?

Still enamored with the idea of giving tours of Chicago, I began searching for other opportunities via Indeed. Eventually I came upon Bobby's Bike Hike, an organization that offered walking, cycling and kayak tours of the city. I immediately nixed the kayaking idea having had an unfortunate experience with the narrow watercraft when I was twelve and having no interest in reliving it in front of paying customers.

But the company also offered numerous walking tours ranging from Chinatown to the burgeoning West Side. Some tours involved food stops. Chicago, in my opinion, does not get enough credit for its extraordinary and original dishes. There is more to the city than deep dish pizza.

I applied and, days later, was asked to submit a video audition reel that involved talking about the Great Chicago Fire of 1871. Bobby's provided several talking points but I was free to put my own "spin" on the script, although talking humorously about an event that killed over 300 newly settled residents and destroyed a third of the city seemed inappropriate. Still, I cobbled something together that included a few jokes about Chicago. Two days later, I was told I would be an ideal guide.

For bike tours.

Wait, that wasn't the intention. Leading tourists around a traffic-choked city in the middle of summer, when the population swells with visitors determined, even during an electrical storm, to take selfies in front of a metallic sculpture known as "The Bean," seemed cumbersome. Even downright dangerous. Furthermore, I was slated to give the company's "Bikes, Bites and Brews" tour, one of its most popular - probably because it involved eating pizza and drinking alcohol along the 13-mile route.

What could possibly go wrong?

After a little cajoling from personnel and the promise that I would eventually get to lead walking tours, I agreed to make "Bike Tour Guide" my third side hustle since my separation. Training consisted of accompanying other guides on the tours, where I learned hand signals like "The Bouncing Basketball" which featured me extending my right hand outward and pretending like I was dribbling but, in reality, was telling the group to SLOW DOWN! There was also the "Raise the Roof" signal. This time, palm facing upward, I extended my hand toward the sky in a rapid-fire motion. It's a popular move in hip-hop dance clubs but, on bike tours, it means "Hurry up and pedal through this green light because it's about to turn red and a CTA bus is approaching!"

After three tagalong tours, I was ready to squire my first group around the city solo. On a glorious Sunday afternoon, I met a Chicago couple who had received a Bobby's gift certificate as a wedding gift, and a Swiss duo, honeymooning through America and stopping in Chicago as a midpoint between their Los Angeles and Orlando destinations. Why anybody would choose Disney World as a honeymoon stop is beyond me, but I elected not to share my disdain for the Magic Kingdom with these lovebirds. My wife and children always treated Disney World like customers at an Old Country Buffet, meaning it should be visited as often as possible. I feel every kid should have the opportunity to visit Disney World. Once. After that, step aside and make room for new visitors to visit the Hall of Presidents. Or any other attraction with air conditioning.

My four-person group was small by Bobby's standards; it's not uncommon for this tour to max out at 16 riders. When I had groups of this size, my goal was not so much to humorously regal them with stories about Chicago, but to make sure I didn't lose anybody along the route. That would most likely generate a one-star rating.

Ah yes, the rating system. At 60, I was resigned to knowing my future employment could come down to grades from total strangers. Stars, "likes" and "follows" are today's equivalent of professional success. If a scientist someday develops a cure for cancer, I don't think it will generate much interest unless the news first garners 100,000 "likes" on Facebook. Nevertheless, at each tour's end, I asked my guests to award me five stars if they indeed liked my performance. You're never too old to grovel.

One thing I quickly learned about the difference between walking tours and bicycle tours was that everybody knows how to walk. The same cannot be said of riding a bike. If I didn't know how to swim, I would not sign up for a whitewater rafting excursion. And yet, I encountered numerous guests whose experience riding a two-wheeler was suspect at best. Most of these people were easily identifiable in the first few minutes, when I handed out bikes and told their recipients to "take a quick spin" around the parking lot adjoining the Bobby's Bike Hike office.

"If something doesn't feel right, let me know," I yelled, assuming, incorrectly, that somebody would actually abide by that request. But novice bike riders seem too embarrassed to admit their riding skills are substandard, so they remain silent, despite knowing this tour involves crossing Michigan Avenue, riding north on Rush Street lined with bars and restaurants, and cruising past Wrigley Field. Sometimes DURING Cubs games.

Bobby's also contained a stash of electric bikes, a $30 upgrade. I've never understood the concept of electric bikes; basically you're taking a form of exercise and making it easier. It's like giving marathoners the option of jumping on a moving walkway ten miles into the route and riding it all the way to the finish line. Furthermore, Chicago isn't exactly known for its hills and steep terrain, so an electronic boost is rarely necessary.

I knew I was in trouble when I encountered Sue, a 68-year-old woman from Arizona who was accompanying numerous, younger, family members on a Bikes, Bites and Brews tour. Sue had chosen the electric bike upgrade, meaning she had to get a tutorial from me.

That tutorial consisted of me asking "Have you ever ridden an electric bike before?"

Sue responded negatively.

I launched into Electric Bike 101. "This lever makes it go faster. Just know that these bikes have decent pick up so please don't accelerate unless you have some space in front of you. Why don't you take it for a quick spin around the parking lot?"

Sue jumped on the bike, accelerated…and nearly crashed into a brick wall. I convinced her a battery-free bike was probably a better option. Off we went. Ever the trooper, Sue made it 11 of the 13 miles before declaring she could go no further. Per policy, I locked up her bike, waited while she ordered an Uber and then resumed the tour. Hey, biking isn't for everybody.

Despite these occasional hiccups, I loved my new side hustle. I looked forward to days when my day planner included a tour, sometimes two. Bobby's eventually trained me on walking tours as well, allowing me to learn so much about this loud, dynamic and entertaining city I now called home. When my tours ended and I returned home I felt the same way I feel when I walk offstage after a particularly good comedy performance. I was equally exhausted and energized if that's possible. In fellow guides I had found new friends, some older and some considerably younger. When I wasn't traveling, I had found a way to eliminate boredom and loneliness. My days were becoming happier.

Now it was time to do something about my evenings.

"Your perceived failure can become the catalyst for profound reinvention."

– ***Conan O'Brien*** (Harrington 2018)

K) Single Rizz-ful Male Seeks . . . What Exactly?

A little more about my decision, at 60, to go car-less, a decision I made on my own. Better now than in 20 years, when a relative hides my keys and tells other relatives "Maybe it's time he stops driving. For his own safety."

It was a bittersweet moment I was not prepared for, as a four-wheeled, gas sucking, carbon monoxide-spewing vehicle had been part of my existence since 1984 when I purchased my parents' Oldsmobile Omega with minimal haggling and drove it from Chicago to West Palm Beach, Florida to begin my first job in my adult life. The Omega's hatch was crammed full of clothes, kitchen utensils and little else, for I owned no furniture to speak of. That would come later, mostly via "estate" sales in Palm Beach, home to Mar-A-Lago and dozens of other gargantuan mansions, unnamed and unowned by millionaires with presidential aspirations, but spectacular nonetheless. I didn't exactly pay pennies on the dollar for Buccelatti sterling silver flatware and Tiffany lamps that would accentuate the Bud Light neon beer sign that also made the trip from Chicago. But in one afternoon, I did purchase a kitchen table, two mismatched leather chairs and a floral couch. The couch's previous residence was the Brazilian Court, a seedy hotel turned tourist trap after Robert Kennedy's 28-year-old son David was found dead of a drug overdose there in April 1984. I quizzed management as to the couch's exact location, wondering if perhaps it came from Room 107 where Kennedy took his final breath. No confirmation but that didn't stop me from telling dates I brought back to my apartment that we might be groping one another on a piece of history.

Forty years later, as I drove to the dealership that elected to take my Lincoln Nautilus off my hands, I mentally listed the cars that preceded it, a test any man could ace even if he struggled with more important facts like his wedding anniversary or his kids' birthdays.

In order:

Nissan Sentra

Honda Civic

Oldsmobile Aurora

Pontiac Grand Prix

BMW S5 – Two more would follow the first

Lincoln MKC

Transaction complete, I Ubered back to my condo already wondering if I had made the correct decision. Instead, I took a long walk around my neighborhood, content that my legs would now serve as my primary form of transportation. The longer I walked, the more I realized I was now existing in an environment consisting of men and women half my age, specifically "Gen Z's," born beginning in 1997 and now firmly entrenched in a world where in their opinion, it was perfectly acceptable to bring your dog into a jewelry store, use Venmo to pay for a single item from the Dollar Store, and have full blown conversations on your cell phone from anywhere, including the sauna at my health club. Yes, one day following a workout, clad only in a towel and lost in my own thoughts, I was sitting on one of the wooden benches when a dude walked in mid-Facetime conversation. He was clearly agitated.

"I don't care what Steve wants. I am NOT making that salami!" was his greeting to his Facetime friend and the sauna's other occupants.

Then he left, leading me to wonder if he had a change of heart and would, to Steve's delight, be making the salami. Had he stayed longer, I would have asked him to avoid saying "salami" in a room inhabited by sweaty, mostly naked males.

Did I truly belong here? Not the sauna, but the city. Could I communicate with this demographic? Did I even want to? Or would it be best to call the dealership, insist I made a mistake and ask if it would be possible to purchase my Nautilus back without haggling, drive it to the nearest Florida retirement community – hell, I already knew the route - and ask if any one bedrooms were available?

I knew I needed another person in my life. Yes, I've gone to bars, restaurants, concerts and golf courses solo and have never felt like a leper. I've encountered others who are doing the same, well aware that being in public, alone, no longer carries the stigma it did 20 years ago. But, and I'm not going to lie, eventually it gets old. Everybody gets sick of themselves at some point.

John Kim's book, *Single. On Purpose,* cautions against jumping into a relationship too soon after becoming divorced. Better to date oneself and figure out your own likes, dislikes, quirks and wants before attempting to do so on someone else.

But, he adds, it's not wrong to want friends. And it feels good to be friends with women, without wanting or expecting, anything more.

But where to find these female friends? Despite suggestions to join a club, volunteer, or sign up for a sports league, I was hesitant to do anything that required a calendar commitment. Anybody in the entertainment business, be it actor, musician, comedian, whatever, knows that a new job or opportunity could present itself at any moment. The other members of your golf league will eventually get pissed off when you keep canceling tee times because you have an audition.

Online dating beckoned.

Confession, I had always been intrigued with the idea of finding a match via an internet connection, even when my marriage was at its happiest. That doesn't mean I had a secret account with Ashley Madison, a website that promotes, even encourages, its users to cheat on their spouses via its SUBTLE slogan "Life is short. Have an affair!" (Ashley Madison 2024) In 2015 those users collectively held their breaths, and in the case of men, probably their dicks, when hacking group The Impact Team announced it had infiltrated the site and would begin releasing names and personal information of Ashley Madison clients. True to their word, hackers did release some files although most were emails from Noel Biderman, CEO of Ashley Madison's parent company, Avid Life Media. The scandal blew over, more or less, and today Ashley Madison remains. For confirmation, I just typed ashleymadison.com into my web browser.

With algorithms and "Big Brother is Watching" technology growing more sophisticated by the day, I can't wait to see what my email inbox and social media sites will contain in the coming weeks.

Online dating wasn't a thing when I met my ex because the internet wasn't yet a thing. If your initial encounter with a mate wasn't face to face, it could only occur via a personal ad, usually found in alternative newspapers. While living in Chicago in the early 1990s, I used to eagerly await Thursday evenings, as the weekly, and free, *Chicago Reader* hit street receptacles and certain bars and retail establishments. I cared little about articles spotlighting Chicago's thriving art and theatre scene; instead, like most fans of *The Reader*, I immediately flipped to the publication's rear so I could imagine the person behind ads like "Single, fun female, 32, seeks like-minded man of same for dating, hanging out and possibly more. No drama queens or vegans, please."

The Missed Connections posts were even more entertaining:

I saw you on the Brown Line L at approximately 2:37 p.m on October 14. You were reading Bonfire of the Vanities. At one point I thought you were looking at me. Respond only if that was really you and you were in fact looking at me.

If you two got together and ultimately married, can you please contact me? Because I really want to know how your situation turned out.

It was inevitable that my ex and I met in a comedy club. In 1991, smoky rooms containing lone microphones, weathered chairs in front of slightly raised wooden platforms and names like "Uncle Funny's" were where I spent most of my existence.

Uncle Funny's was an actual club in South Florida where I began my career. There were so many clubs in the early '90s that owners were doing anything to stand out from the competition, including giving their establishments names that were anything but funny. "The Comedy Clinic," a short-lived club in Deerfield Beach, Florida, comes to mind. The club's desire to equate laughs with a "cure" for whatever ailed patrons was met with ridicule by the South Florida Sun-Sentinel, the Fort Lauderdale area's most popular newspaper, which offered this assessment in a 1989 review:

Want an evening of laughter in plush surroundings, with lovingly prepared food and an inviting atmosphere? Then visit The Comedy Clinic only in an emergency. At this point, this is a Band-Aid nightclub.

The review failed to mention if the club could resuscitate a comedian who was "dying" on stage. (Brazer 2021)

I first encountered my wife at K.J. Riddles Comedy Club. The "K" and the "J" represented the owners, Ken and John. I'm not sure why they tacked on "Riddles" as it implies the customer is not sure what awaits him or her upon entering the premises. K and J had met while co-managing Catch a Rising Star, a chain comedy club with an offshoot in the Hyatt Regency Chicago, possibly the worst setting for humor. Popular with conventioneers, the audience mostly consisted of middle-aged men, sitting alone and nursing expense-account drinks, oblivious to the fact they were still wearing convention name badges that screamed "I HAVE SPENT THE ENTIRE DAY AT THE NATIONAL FLOOR LAMP EXPO! AND MY NAME IS STAN!"

The duo chose a south suburban Chicago strip mall for their new venture, and one with the most unlikely entrance procedure. Patrons parked in the mall's rear and walked through a large, drafty lobby featuring a popcorn machine and the offices of K and J. Despite signage saying "box office this way" and an arrow confirming its existence, customers almost always passed it by, returning only upon realizing they needed tickets before entering the showroom.

I did the same thing the first time I worked the club. Arriving half an hour before the doors officially opened, I was headed to the showroom in search of K, J or popcorn when I heard a female voice over my right shoulder.

"Can I help you?"

Turning, I noticed the box office and the occupant inside.

"No, I'm one of the comics," I replied.

"Oh wow, another comic too good to talk to the hired help," my eventual wife said.

Obviously, we began talking. After I had wiped the verbal blood from my nose.

Had dating sites been around during that initial box office encounter, I wonder if my ex and I would have struck up a conversation at all? Using technology to find a match just seemed so…easy. Even if you felt you had zero personal communication skills – if the idea of "selling" yourself, face to face, to a stranger who you found physically and emotionally enticing terrified you - the same thing could be done, with extreme confidence, using a computer.

And oh, the choices!

Just as bottled water devolved from a single brand to dozens separating themselves as "artesian," "purified," "mineral," and "electrolyte boosted," so did dating sites. The more people embraced dating sites, the more segmented those sites became. In 2023, Broadbandsearch.net estimated more than 44.2 million users in the United States alone were using approximately 8,000 dating sites. There are sites for golfers, cigar smokers, tattoo lovers and pickleball players. One day I stumbled across a site for those who shun gluten. Two of the most attractive, airbrushed people I had ever seen were smiling on the home page, their expressions saying "I have FINALLY found somebody who, like me, won't eat bagels!"

I wanted to smack them both with a frozen loaf of French bread and then toss their unconscious bodies into a pot of boiling wheat pasta.

Nonetheless, with this kind of availability, it's a wonder anybody is home alone on a Saturday night.

Still separated, and realizing there was no hope for a reconciliation, I vowed I would never be lonely. Instead, I would plunge headfirst into this cyber world that, up until now, I had only encouraged others to try, never mind that I had no experience in it myself.

"Why aren't you online dating?" I would ask single friends and even my oldest daughter. Looking back, I admit it was very judgmental of me; perhaps my daughter was patiently waiting to hear back from her "Missed Connection."

Jason, a cycling club friend from my old neighborhood and mired in his own divorce, was my knowledge source for all cyberdating-related questions. Jason had tried multiple sites, a few simultaneously, yet judging by his stories he had met with limited success. But I wondered, what was the definition of success? Jason seemed to want partners for sex, as most of his stories about matches concluded with whether or not he got laid. Match.com he emphatically stated, was the best site for that.

Other stories ended much like the "...and then COVID hit" conclusion covered in a previous chapter.

"...and then she told me she had a kid."

"...and then she decided to go back with her husband."

...and then I realized she just wanted money."

I knew some of these finales awaited me if I chose to meet women online. I also wondered if it was too early to take the plunge seeing that my wife and I were separated but not even close to a divorce. Maybe that's because I had neglected to hire the attorney employed by ANOTHER friend in the midst of divorcing who, after listening to my saga over a single half hour Zoom call, said "Based on what I'm hearing, I think I can have you divorced in 30 days."

"Let me guess" I thought after hearing that bout of braggadocio. "Your rates are 50 percent off. TODAY ONLY!"

Shunning caution from some friends who thought yes, it was too early, I chose eHarmony as my dating platform. I paid $350 for a yearlong membership and began creating my profile, a process that lasted longer than some of my college courses. Also, some marriages.

eHarmony was, according to Jason, more suited for people seeking long term relationships than one-night stands. eHarmony begs to differ, as the home page contains a series of questions, one of which is "What kind of a relationship are you looking for?" The choices were 'Casual,' 'Serious' or 'Not Sure, Just Browsing.' While I contemplated my selection, my eyes went to a declaration on the site's lower third:

"Every 14 minutes, someone finds love on eHarmony."

What, I wondered, was eHarmony's definition of love? And how exactly were those statistics compiled? Had eHarmony achieved the listening skills of, say, TikTok? It's been suggested, even proven, according to some social media experts, that China, where TikTok originated, is using the platform to spy on unwitting users. I'll vouch for that; one day after deciding to take a day hike in Alaska and texting a fellow comedian/hiker for suggestions, my TikTok feed was filled with videos of hikers encountering bears. I don't know what I would do if a grizzly ever appeared on my hiking trail but it would not involve whipping out my iPhone and experimenting with the camera's telephoto feature.

I chose "casual," said I was a man looking for a woman, as opposed to seeking a man or a non-binary individual and began the tedious process of completing the 80-question compatibility quiz. And no, 80 is not a typo. The site claims 20 minutes is sufficient time to complete the quiz but encourages users to "take a break!"

It's been nearly a year since I took the quiz, so I can't remember my exact answers to questions like "Are You Open To Meeting a Person Who Already Has Children?" I believe I responded "Yes, as long as that child is not of Little League age because, at 60, I have no interest in being the guy who looks like he would be more at home in a lawn chair down the left field line than coaching third base."

"How happy are you with your physical appearance?"

That one was easy: "Depends on whether the previous night out with friends included tequila."

"How far should we search for your matches?"

That one I pondered for a moment. I knew when I signed up that I would soon uproot myself from the comforts of my suburban surroundings of almost 30 years and relocate to the city of Chicago. I had already begun interviewing potential realtors. Therefore, I wanted to meet matches who lived in the city. So, for me, eHarmony would be more of a fact-finding app. Were women close to my age happy being single in a city of 3 million people? Was there enough to do? I know that sounds strange; why wouldn't there be enough to do? However, one realizes very quickly that city living requires being in decent shape. It's not like the suburbs, where residents just get in their cars and finds parking spots close to whatever bank, restaurant, church or Costco is on their daily agenda. Want to get around quickly in Chicago? Invest in a good pair of walking shoes because you're gonna need 'em.

I set "less than 15 miles" from the city limit as my search parameters. I also told eHarmony I was only interested in meeting women between 50 and 65. Sex maniac Jason was flabbergasted.

I created my profile, careful not to let details of my personal situation infiltrate it. I knew there was a chance my wife could see it, as she has single and divorced friends who are probably exploring the online dating scene as well. No sense in beginning sentences with "I'm here because my wife and I…(INSERT SOB STORY HERE)

I researched, online of course, what to include in an online profile. While doing so, I came across an unfamiliar word that was attracting lots of attention.

Rizz. The Oxford University Press 2023 word of the year. (Syed 2023)

The esteemed British institution, whose alums include Sir Walter Raleigh and Rupert Murdoch, also is famous for, since 2004, anointing a "word of the year." According to OUP, the word is chosen based on the "ethos, mood, or preoccupations of that particular year and to have lasting potential as a word of cultural significance." In 2013 that word was "selfie." Even my 88-year-old mother has used that one.

The initial winner was "chav," a British term used to describe an anti-social lower-class youth dressed in sportswear.

The next year, seemingly unable to make a universal decision, the university chose "sudoku" as its' UK word and "podcast" as its US word of the year. Both endure to this day; I'm not sure if there are still chavs running around England 20 years after being outed by Oxford.

Rizz, short for "charisma," and defined as the ability to charm and woo a person, bested "Swiftie," "situationship" and "de-influencing" to claim the 2023 title. I had heard "Swiftie" thrown around during the year as it pertains to those so obsessed by pop star Taylor Swift that they will fly halfway around the world to score her concert tickets, and cause traffic snarls three days before one of her shows by standing for that amount of time in a merch line to purchase an $80 Taylor T-shirt.

"De-influencing" I discovered, is when a social media influencer tells his or her legion of followers NOT to buy certain products. Once I heard that definition, I immediately vowed to become one so I could tell people not to purchase Taylor Swift T-shirts. It would greatly reduce my time in traffic.

"Situationship" awaits most people exploring online dating for it is defined as "a romantic or intimate relationship that lacks clear definitions or commitments typically associated with traditional romantic relationships." Sounds like a lot of marriages I've observed over the years.

I'm not sure why Oxford gets to choose the word; I've been to Oxford University and I couldn't understand what anybody was saying, even though that may be due to my difficulty in deciphering strong English accents. That's why I quickly lost interest in *Ted Lasso.* It's also why I will probably never date a British lady; constantly saying "Can you repeat that?" is hardly rizz-like.

Rizz seemed like a perfect word to include in my online dating profile. "Funny, athletic and unlimited rizz" should generate some "likes" and "swipe rights" from members of the opposite sex.

One would think.

Instead, I opted for simple, honest sentences.

I am getting divorced at 60 but feel like there is so much life still to live and I plan to do that. Right now I am looking for new people to hang out with. If that's you, then let's hang out.

I started with the free listing but quickly upgraded to what should be called the "Your Ego Needs Stroking" listing. Under eHarmony's free plan, one can message a finite number of potential matches but can't see their profile photos, which appear blurry next to their responses. I wanted to SEE what these women who responded to my prose looked like. Otherwise, what was the point?

I also vowed to take a proactive approach. Rather than wait for potential matches to come to me, I elected to reach out to women who caught my eye, now that they were no longer blurry. First off was Judy, a human resources administrator who seemed incapable of taking a decent photograph. She had uploaded three images of herself, all of which looked like she was pissed that she had even signed up for eHarmony. And yet, she was a long-time city resident, divorced with no kids and we shared a few common interests.

What the hell?

We began cyberchatting and, after the normal small talk, I asked if she would like to meet at a Starbucks in Chicago's Lakeview neighborhood. Online dating would not exist were it not for the coffee giant. The next time you enter a Starbucks look around. Every patron is probably working on their screenplay or meeting a cyberdate for the first time.

Judy and I talked for over an hour. She told me that yes, she was perfectly comfortable living in Chicago and couldn't imagine residing anywhere else. She liked music, theatre, the occasional museum and just about any ethnic food placed in front of her. I quizzed her on health insurance plans, knowing she was in HR and I would soon be kicked off my wife's plan. We parted ways and agreed to stay in touch. Returning to my car, I felt all the emotions I assume one feels after having a lengthy conversation with a member of the opposite sex who is not your spouse. It was both strange and invigorating, the latter being enough for me to think this online dating scene might be a perfect and immediate cure for loneliness and lack of friends.

Online dating is like sidling up to a buffet you know contains all your favorite dishes, but you must look for them. Also, those crab claws you stumbled on and heaped heavily onto your plate might not taste exactly how you would prefer, although they *looked* delicious. After taking the eHarmony plunge, I immediately began scrolling through the profiles of Chicago women who looked, in the buffet line anyway, worth contacting. My strategy was to view their pictures and then comment on something in the background. I asked Lisa what game she was attending since I noticed goalposts behind her. After hitting "send," I concluded I was actually looking at a yellow structural beam of some sort. Lisa never replied, probably realizing I had no understanding of sports. Or construction.

Randi chose a photo that looked as it could easily have landed on her debut album cover were she a pop singer as opposed to a "hypnotherapist/business owner." Her pic featured her paddleboarding towards a sunset so fiery red. I assumed she lived on the planet Mercury, or at least an Uber ride away from it. I tried paddleboarding once and hated it, although I would be willing to give it another try in Randi's environment. She reached out to me by sending an ice cream bar emoji, eHarmony's definition of an "icebreaker." Clicking the bar leads the user to a series of five "either or" photos, the idea being to see if your choices agree with your connection's tastes.

I took her bait and began the test. First was a photo of what appeared to be an expensive European hotel next to what could best be described as a "cottage in the country." I guess eHarmony wanted to know where I would rather vacation. I chose the hotel.

Next up were what looked like two paint swatches. I felt like I had just been transported to a Home Depot to contemplate what color to paint the guest room. One was a coarse gray while the other was a smooth beige.

What the hell was the point of this? Do couples get together or worse, split up, because one likes beige and the other doesn't? To continue the quiz I chose gray, probably sending eHarmony's algorithms into overdrive.

He prefers gray? We NEVER would have guessed that!

Picture three showed a hand holding a pencil and working the 2005 word of the year, a Sudoku puzzle. The other picture was of a half-completed jigsaw puzzle. I couldn't choose "neither" so I went with jigsaw.

It was about this time that I thought of my parents, happily married for 53 years even though Mom liked jigsaw puzzles and Dad did not. Would a site like eHarmony have kept them from meeting, falling in love, getting married and staying together until death did in fact part them? Being TOO compatible is not necessarily a good thing. I mean, I wouldn't want to date myself, despite John Kim's suggestion. I'm not THAT interesting. Plus, I snore. I forged on.

Number four showed a couple in an art gallery, their backs to the camera, staring intently at a series of watercolors, alongside a photo of a man crowd surfing, yes, CROWD SURFING, at what I assumed was a concert. Either that or a Thanksgiving family gathering that went off the rails. I'm not an art aficionado by any means but I also have no interest in meeting women over 50 who use whatever means necessary to score a better vantage point at Coachella. I chose the art gallery.

My final choice was most confusing. Picture one showed a woman with her head sticking out of the car she was driving. She had pulled onto the shoulder and was staring at a road leading towards snowcapped mountains. She was also holding a map that, upon closer inspection, contained a narrow strip of land surrounded by bodies of water. I love mountains but did I want a mate who was hopelessly lost or, at the least, "directionally challenged?" I opted for the alternative - two tropical drinks on a table between two empty lounge chairs overlooking an infinity pool with a tranquil sea just beyond. I think it was where the woman in the car was trying to get to before she made a seriously wrong turn. The empty chairs were the only reason I didn't cancel my eHarmony membership immediately, as I assumed they were empty because the occupants, who met on eHarmony, had found an abandoned stretch of beach and were having wild, rizzful sex.

Upon completing the survey, eHarmony said I scored a 78 percent match with Randi. Shortly thereafter I received a message from her:

"Hey Greg. Brand new to eHarmony. I have no idea what I just did. Lol. Did you have a fun weekend?"

I did but I wasted most of it taking an insipid compatibility test. I neglected to mention this but, seeing that Randi lived more than 150 miles from Chicago, I elected to send her paddleboarding into the sunset.

More scrolling, texting and, in some cases, meetups followed. There was Viv, a nonprofit executive who I met at an independently owned coffee shop (Sorry Starbucks) on a rainy Sunday after church. The collagen in her lips could have filled a Macy's Thanksgiving Day balloon. Viv took exactly one sip of her coffee before revealing she had been sober for five years and also was the victim of an abusive relationship. I decided it wasn't to be, even if she liked jigsaw puzzles.

Kate and I, after some initial texting, agreed to chat via Zoom. She sent me the link to her personal Zoom meeting room; I logged on at the agreed upon time and was greeted with the following message:

"Welcome to Grandma Kate's meeting room. You are the first participant."

GRANDMA Kate joined a few seconds after, but it was too late. Yes, some women over 50 are grandmas but no need to announce it. Via Zoom. We chatted for a few minutes, but she too lived a hefty distance from me and I knew it would go nowhere.

Mind you, it wasn't always me making the decision on whether to move forward. WARNING! Do not attempt online dating unless you can handle rejection without ever discovering why said rejection occurred. All online dating sites should include this disclaimer, even Ashley Madison.

Case in point: Shortly after my initial encounter with Judy, I noticed Sarah's profile. A light-haired brunette with a beautiful smile, she was divorced, living in the city after years in the suburbs and, like me, an avid Pickleball player and fan of the HBO shitshow *White Lotus.* Sarah was more than happy to give her opinions on owning a car in the city ("I have one but mostly use it for Costco runs"), where to find Pickleball partners ("I joined a group with 1,600 players!") and the over 50 dating pool in the city versus the suburbs ("From a dating aspect there might be more people in the 'burbs in our age group and people shy away from dating someone in the city. But then I think, do I want to be with someone who doesn't enjoy the vibrancy and activities Chicago offers?")

Sarah's calendar seemed more cluttered than mine, and I travel for a living. It wasn't until nearly two months after we first connected that we met at a bar in Roscoe Village, a very family-oriented neighborhood on Chicago's northwest side. When I arrived, she was already at the bar, a craft beer in front of her.

An excellent start, I thought.

Our conversation was, basically, an extension of our online chats. Stories about Pickleball, transportation, desirable city neighborhoods, our respective careers and where to meet over 50 singles kept us at the bar for about 90 minutes. At one point, she asked the status of my divorce. I held firm to my goal of not discussing my issues, be they legal or personal, during a first meeting. Why muddy the waters when meeting someone new?

Someone who piques your curiosity? As one ages, there are fewer chances to encounter new individuals and hear their stories. Online dating increases those odds.

Glancing at my watch, I apologized that the afternoon, now stretching into evening, had to end. I was catching a flight to Ecuador the following morning and hadn't even begun packing. We agreed to continue the conversation, in person and in another part of the city.

Walking Sarah to her car (she had driven to the bar, so I was apparently as worthy as a Costco run) I felt like a high school sophomore walking a girl to her front door after our first date, if you want to call hanging out at the mall a "date." Do I hug her? Kiss her? Do the COVID thing and fist bump her?

As I contemplated all the choices, Sarah stopped as we approached her vehicle, wrapped her arms around my waist, planted a light kiss on my lips and told me what a wonderful time she had.

Thank you, eHarmony!

I never saw or heard from Sarah again.

Fuck you, eHarmony!

At 60, I was left to ponder why I had been so mysteriously dumped? I replayed our bar conversation continuously. Was I wrong in keeping details of my divorce private? Did that mean I didn't value her opinion? Should I have made sure I arrived at the bar before her? I wasn't late by any means but maybe she felt uncomfortable sitting by herself. Did I drink my beer too slowly? ("He's boring"). Too quickly? ("He's an alcoholic!")

Tom, my best comedian friend, heard my story but didn't seem surprised.

"I've never tried online dating myself, but I can't tell you how many friends have told me the exact same story," he said.

With my ego and confidence plummeting, I dragged myself back to the eHarmony buffet. Where I spied Sandra.

She was a petite, some might say uncomfortably skinny, dark-haired woman who had posted several pictures with non-descript backgrounds. No photos of attending Cubs games, standing under a waterfall in a South American rainforest or holding a full glass of wine. The latter, incidentally, seems to be the most popular eHarmony selfie among females. If I couldn't find a woman on a dating site, I vowed to move to Napa.

From her profile, I saw we shared an alma mater in Northwestern University. That became the primary subject in our initial chats, which occurred during the March Madness NCAA basketball tournament. After a lengthy hiatus, Northwestern had returned to the tournament in 2023. One night I picked up my phone as the Wildcats were embroiled in a tight contest.

"Are you watching this?" I texted

"I am now," she responded.

"Would you like to meet for coffee? At Starbucks?"

"Sure."

We chose a Starbucks less than half a mile from the Judy encounter. Still living in the suburbs, I made the 45-minute car ride on a gray Sunday but one with temperatures that showed hints of Spring. Restaurants and coffee shops alike were beginning to reassemble outdoor seating area and urging patrons to dine al fresco even if it meant doing so in winter coats.

As I walked toward the Starbucks, Sandra texted that she had already arrived and would happily order for me.

"Tall nonfat latte," was my response.

I found her sitting outside with two cups and looking disappointed that all the indoor seating was occupied. I tried lightening the mood.

"Good thing I'm a 'Simple Starbucks order' type of guy," I said. "If I texted you the drink my kids usually order, you'd still be scrolling."

Sandra dropped her head, clasped her hands together and began to laugh. Only that's not how it appeared to me. With her head shaking, shoulders heaving and her gaze downward. I thought she was in the initial throes of a seizure. Not exactly the ideal first impression.

How was your first date, Greg?

The first 90 seconds were great! Then the ambulance arrived.

Eventually I realized that was her way of expressing joy. Some people loudly snort when they laugh; others achieve hilarity without making a sound.

Sandra seized.

Just as I realized she wasn't going to die in front of me, a single gentleman left his table, probably because his online date never showed. Or he'd finished his screenplay. We took his spot and began a lengthy and delightful conversation. Sandra was 63, widowed and winding down a long and successful career as a criminal defense attorney. In between her stories, I regaled her with a few from my early days as a newspaper and television reporter in West Palm Beach. My beat included the criminal court system, so I had seen, firsthand, the challenges of defending everyone from perverted lowlifes to politicians with penchants for getting behind the wheel after alcohol-fueled fundraisers, to rock legend David Crosby, who sat among career criminals in prison garb after walking into a West Palm Beach police station in December 1985 and saying "I give up." Crosby, strung out from years of freebasing, was wanted on weapons charges in Texas when he surrendered.

Sandra seemed enthralled, leading me to think none of her other eHarmony dates had firsthand knowledge of the criminal defense system.

"Who was your favorite client?" I asked.

"There was this one guy who I just loved," she said. "Granted he was a mass murderer, but he was always honest and upfront with me. That's what I loved about him."

Talk about low standards!

She told me about her city upbringing, and about her dad who failed to show at her wedding despite a friendly phone conversation the evening prior. Sandra eventually walked herself down the aisle.

She'd named her dog Atticus, after Atticus Finch from *To Kill a Mockingbird.* She was an avid swimmer, rising before dawn to commandeer a lane at her health club. Swimming was occasionally a part of my early morning workouts too, but Sandra clearly enjoyed it more. We left the Starbucks and headed for Chicago's lakefront, where we spent an hour among the Sunday runners and bikers only too eager to enjoy this burst of Spring with us.

Two weeks later, I sat with Sandra in the courtyard of her building, a luxury hi-rise on Lake Shore Drive, sipping cabernet and snacking from a charcuterie board featuring creations she had whipped up. Now I felt comfortable sharing details of my divorce. I shed some tears. She listened, squeezed my hand a few times and offered encouragement. Eventually I revealed my realtor had found a place she thought was perfect for me, a hi-rise condominium unit close to where Sandra resided.

And when I say close, I mean thisclose. Like, close enough to open my window and yell "I'LL BE OVER IN FIVE MINUTES! DO I NEED A JACKET?"

Thus began my first relationship in thirty years, albeit still platonic, with a woman not my wife. I settled into my new digs and our courtyard wine and cheese forays became more frequent. She revealed she had only recently entered the online dating pool, feeling doing so too quickly would show lack of respect, or compassion, for her late husband.

And here is where I began to realize that being out of the dating pool for more than a quarter century means mistakes are bound to happen. The first, according to a woman I met online months later, involved inviting Sandra to a concert with new friends, along with my cousin and her husband. Big mistake, the friend told me. Never mix new friends of the opposite sex with relatives.

"That gave her the impression you wanted your family's approval," the friend said.

At the concert, Sandra seized the opportunity, working the group and chatting amiably with my cousin who pulled me aside about two hours into the evening.

"She's really into you."

"How so?" I asked.

"She said she's going to be the first woman to share your bed in your new place."

"She said THAT?"

I was convinced my cousin was joking or had heard Sandra incorrectly. Criminal defense attorneys don't make statements like that for fear of hearing "OBJECTION!" from the other side.

I shrugged it off. May turned into June and we were still seeing one another but, true to my profile, I still considered us to be in "hangout" mode. She introduced me to some of her favorite restaurants, accompanied me to a free symphonic concert at Chicago's scenic Pritzker Pavilion, and attended a neighborhood art festival. Our mutual love of street fairs led to another afternoon festival, this one in the West Loop. For weeks Sandra had been talking about the VIP tickets she had purchased, allowing us to sit in a tented area, drink and eat for free and basically stay clear of the thousands of Gen Z's, strollers and dogs who attend street fairs in the Windy City.

When we arrived, none of those promises panned out. There was no free food or liquid libations to speak of. Yes, we found the tent, but we were the only ones sitting beneath it, looking like two people who paramedics parked there because they were suffering from heat exhaustion.

Sandra's mood soured. It continued when we returned to her place, about 7 p.m. The night was still young, but I sensed she wanted to end it. Something was clearly bothering her.

I began verbally probing a lawyer, probably not the best idea.

"Did you have fun today?"

"Of course I did," she said.

"OK, it just seemed like you had something on your mind."

"No, I'm fine. Really. I always have fun when we're together."

"I agree," I said. "You're such a great friend."

"Mm-hmm."

"No, you really are," I said. "You're exactly what I've been looking for at this point in my life. In fact, I'd like to have about ten of you."

OBJECTION!

Recounting the story later, the friend who chided me for mixing dating with family was even more brutal in her assessment.

"You might as well have said 'I'm forming a harem and I'd like you to join.'"

"I thought I was being honest," I said.

Sandra thought otherwise. We parted ways with our typical hug and mutual peck on the lips and I walked home. Remember, I lived only about 400 yards from her; the text that awaited me as I entered my condo and checked my phone obviously hadn't taken long to construct.

"Greg, I don't think we should see each other anymore. I'm looking for a relationship. I have enough friends."

I was hurt. Not because Sandra had dumped me but because I had been dumped period. I wasn't a big dater in high school or college but could never recall a woman telling me she wanted me out of her life. Well, unless you count my divorce.

Maybe she overreacted. Two weeks later I tested that theory by sending Sandra a text from Alaska, where I had boarded another cruise ship. Stopping in a souvenir store in Ketchikan, a town that proclaims itself "THE SALMON CAPITAL OF THE WORLD," I snapped a photo of an Ulu knife, a half moon-shaped weapon that Quentin Tarantino will probably find use for in his next movie. Not only was she a defense attorney who found mass murderers appealing, but Sandra confided as I watched her cut cheese one evening, she also was a huge fan of knives.

She neglected to include either of those facts on her eHarmony profile.

"Happy to bring you one of these," I texted. "As long as TSA thinks it's OK."

No response.

It was indeed over. Back to the eHarmony buffet.

But not right away. I reverted to the advice from Kim's book about working on myself before plunging back into the dating pool. A friend introduced me to a fellow golf lover, and we played a few times at the city course adjacent to my condo. I took long walks along the lake, sometimes with Airpods and sometimes without. I found a church I felt comfortable in. I convinced myself I was happy with myself.

But I wasn't. My time with Sandra revealed that I enjoyed companionship. I returned to eHarmony and, after a few scrolls, found Rachel. Her profile pic featured her seated on the shores of Lake Michigan, the Chicago skyline visible in the background. No dog or glass of Pinot Grigio accompanied her. She was alone and smiling. I was intrigued.

True to my plan of commenting on something within the photo, I messaged her:

"Did you take that pic before or after you went sailing?"

The response came a few hours later.

"LOL, I don't sail. But I do like to walk along the lake."

That was enough for me. Over the next few days, we messaged back and forth before I asked if we could get together for a drink.

"Let's talk on the phone first," she replied.

I immediately gave her my number, although sites such as eHarmony discourage revealing too much personal information. Rachel didn't seem to care though.

"Let me call you," she said.

Three days later, when the phone rang at our agreed upon time, my screen said "PRIVATE." At least it was better than GRANDMA KATE!

We chatted for over an hour about her job as a graphic artist for a large Chicago advertising firm, her divorce and a not-so-great online dating/stalking experience, which explained her unwillingness to reveal her phone number, for now anyway.

Once I deduced she was happy with the way the conversation was going, I asked if we could meet in person.

"Did I pass the test?" I asked.

"Oh yes," she replied. "You're definitely not a psycho."

We opted not for a Starbucks but for a bar in Andersonville, a trendy north side neighborhood known for attracting artists, independent store owners and affluent members of the gay community. I arrived 15 minutes early, determined not to make her sit by herself.

I still wasn't sure if that was the reason Sarah blew me off.

Rachel arrived at exactly 6 p.m. She ordered her first drink, while I ordered my second. If she was perturbed that I'd started drinking without her, it didn't show. Our conversation never lapsed into silence; she even suggested we order another drink.

We opted to end the evening after that, without food. But, as we were leaving, I suggested another meeting.

"You never told me what kind of food you like," I said. "Where do you like to eat?"

"I'm up for anything."

"Love hearing that," I said, before adding, "I can walk you home or we can part ways here and I can jump on the next bus back to my neighborhood."

"I think I'll just walk," she said.

We parted ways. I waited two days before messaging her, which was difficult for I couldn't wait to talk to her again. I also sensed she was everything Sandra was not when it came to wanting to hang out versus wanting to share my bed.

Finally, I could wait no longer.

"Hey, I know your schedule is crazy. Just wondering how much lead time you need before we make a dinner date."

The response was quick and to the point.

"Hi Greg. I had a great time with you, but I just didn't feel a connection. Thank you for a lovely evening."

Boom. Dumped again. At least Sandra had provided some explanation. But Rachel? She extended our time together, opened up about her past, even suggested a few of her favorite restaurants…and STILL didn't feel anything? What was it going to take?

I decided that if I were to continue meeting strange women online, be it to hang out or take the next step, I was going to have to do some probing of my own, as opposed to being the "probe-ee" so to speak.

It was either that or slit my wrists.

I'm kidding of course. Remember, I never did purchase the Ulu knife.

"I poured spot remover on my dog. Now he's gone."

– Attributed to Steven Wright (BrainyMedia 2024)

L) At My Bar Dogs Will Drink for Free

When you spend more than 50 percent of the year on the road, and you're a sexagenarian, your thought process often involves a series of numbers.

I've visited 49 of the 50 states; performed in 48 of them. I'm a 3-million-mile American Airlines flier. I have visited Las Vegas 112 times. My record for steps in one day is 30,645.

I've lost track of the number of bars I've frequented.

I am not an alcoholic but, for me, a successful road trip usually includes discovery of a good bar, tavern, pub, watering hole, microbrewery, whatever you want to call it. Other than a gambling table, it is the one place where sitting in solitude doesn't bring suspicious or compassionate stares from other patrons wondering "Why is this guy alone?"

I walk a lot so sometimes the bars come to me. I can't explain exactly what draws me in. Often it's the location; a "corner bar" is more than a generic description for me. Place a bar at the right angle of two intersecting streets, stick at least one neon beer sign in the window – but no more than five – and your establishment will most likely get a visit from me. I might not stay long; I will survey the place and leave if the surroundings are not to my liking or, specifically, if the bar violates the Schwem Doctrine:

- The bar must contain at least three patrons.
- None can be wearing a MAGA hat or any article of clothing praising a certain president who shall not be named.
- *Wheel of Fortune* must not be on the bar TV. Worse, the patrons cannot be actively yelling their guesses.
- The bar cannot and will not ever partake in karaoke or trivia nights.

If your bar passes that preliminary test, I will commandeer a stool. I don't care if you're male, female, young, old, straight, gay, single or married. I don't care if you're with friends. I don't care if there is one lone stool left and I get an eye roll when I ask "Is anybody sitting here?" and squeeze myself in even though the adjoining patrons were hoping for a little extra space. Or pretending to save it by placing an article of clothing on the stool.

Once seated, I will order what always used to be a beer although my ongoing battle with gluten has caused me to experiment with other liquid libations. I can drink a tap cider but gesturing to the bartender and saying "Another cider please" just doesn't have the same effect as pointing to an empty beer mug. Beer drinkers don't even have to speak; they merely point and a good bartender will refill their mugs with nary a word. Is it any wonder that beer is the world's third most popular beverage, water and tea taking the top two spots? That's right coffee drinkers;

BEER is preferred more than the Starbucks venti vanilla sweet cream cold brew with exactly two Splenda packets that you crave enough to stand in an airport line for 35 minutes, never mind that your flight is boarding.

If you're a beer drinker, chances are you might get a free one, as beer drinkers tend to buy beers for one another. The same cannot be said of wine drinkers. Ever ask a wine drinker when heading to the bar what they wish to drink? The answer will never be short.

"Ask the bartender if he has a Syrah, fruity but not sweet, from the upper Napa Valley region" was the last response I received when I asked a friend, exclusively a wine drinker, what he'd like.

"I have a better idea" I said. "How about you ask him that? And while you're up there, can you grab me a beer?"

See how that works?

While some bar patrons prefer to drink or dine in solitude, such is not the case with me. Yes, I am a comedian, but I am first and foremost, a conversationalist. That means I will do my best to get a fellow patron off his or her phone or attempt to draw attention away from the TV. That means keen observation, listening and a willingness to be silent until I make my move. It might involve asking the score of the game they are watching. I have had great conversations and friendly disagreements with fellow patrons once we bonded over sports. I will ask how the food is that my fellow patron just received, wondering if I should order the same thing. Or I will eavesdrop on conversations and insert myself into one when I feel the time is right. Being a comedian helps with this tactic. Make strangers laugh and they are no longer strangers.

COVID took away our conversation and interaction skills and I have found that, with some exceptions, most people are eager to reclaim them. However, that is not always the case. My attempts at conversation have failed with spectacular, sometimes dangerous results. In New Orleans for a speaking engagement in Summer 2022 as lockdown restrictions were easing, I found myself on the second floor of a Bourbon Street establishment. I had passed by earlier and saw four people on the balcony doing what inebriated New Orleans tourists do; gesturing to passerby with half full plastic daiquiri glasses punctuating every sentence with "Wooo!" and just generally letting everybody know the city has fully recovered from not only the pandemic, but also Hurricane Katrina. Still, it looked like it had possibilities and when my friend Alexander turned in for the night, I found myself climbing the steps to see what awaited.

Gone were the "woo-meisters;" in their place sat one couple. I sidled up to the right of the male and waited for a chance to interact. I watched the bartender construct what appeared to be a very complex drink for the man's female companion, consisting of multiple ingredients, garnishes, stirs and shakes. It was definitely a CRAFT cocktail. I saw an opening.

Placing my hand on the man's shoulder I said, "When she's done with that one, I'm gonna order the same thing."

He turned, placed his index finger on my left temple, applied pressure and said "Don't ever fucking touch me again."

I checked my watch, hoping *Wheel of Fortune* was about to start.

I said nothing. His date looked at her shoes. The female bartender sensing trouble looked at me as she continued mixing. "Sir, I'm going to have to ask you to leave."

I caught her strategy. She wasn't asking me to leave because I was causing a commotion; rather she was asking me to leave before the psycho whose space I had just invaded turned violent.

I left, careful not to mutter anything under my breath or even turn back, for I could feel the guy's eyes boring into me. Sadly, we live in a society where guns are as prevalent on our persons as house keys. I learned my lesson. No touching.

I will admit, when I've had a few drinks and bar conversation is rolling along nicely, my hands occasionally wander. I've been accused of hitting on my fellow patrons, both male and female, although my gestures are purely platonic. But I have learned it's best to keep my hands to myself, lest I become the object of a two-star Yelp review that reads: "It's a great place but I had to leave after I was groped by some creepy guy from Chicago. He said he was a comedian, but I didn't find him funny."

Yelp, incidentally, has been a great source of bar finds. Once, while walking in San Francisco, I typed "dive bars" into the search engine and was directed to Northstar Café, nestled in the city's North Beach neighborhood and just three minutes away from my hotel. Once inside, I noticed a single gentleman, early 30s, staring intently at the Philadelphia Flyers hockey game onscreen.

"Flyers fan?" I asked.

"You know it." You?"

"Nope but I'm a hockey fan. After all, I do live in Chicago. It's kind of the law right now."

I was alluding to the heyday of the Chicago Blackhawks which won three Stanley cups in six years and, in the process, depleted the savings accounts of most suburban Chicago parents with boys, all of whom suddenly wanted to be the next Patrick Kane or Jonathan Toews. Parents, if your kid wants to play hockey, just remember that he will need new skates every six months. Start adding up the investment now and then encourage him to take up swimming before you are forced to acquire second jobs and mortgages. Arms and legs don't need replacing. Also, bathing suits are cheaper than goalie pads.

His name was Chris and he laughed at my Chicago hockey reference. Mission accomplished. From there, we talked hockey, sports, and life for about two hours. I learned he was a Philly native but took a job in San Francisco and was enjoying the city although his roots were pulling him back. We exchanged cell phone numbers and LinkedIn profiles. When I returned to the city by the Bay a year later, he was still there. We met at another bar, had dinner and then caught up. He has since returned to Philadelphia, gotten married, had one child and admitted in a recent email that life wasn't as rosy as that last sentence. I don't get to Philly often but, when I do, Chris will be the first person I call.

Such is the beauty of bar conversations.

When it comes to communication, I have often found airport bars to be tops on the list. Most airport bar customers are traveling solo and, while the majority are scrolling their phones, they seem eager to converse with strangers. Think about it…when you walk into an airport bar you already have something in common with every other patron; you are traveling…somewhere. Furthermore, if you're in the bar and not at your gate, chances are your flight is delayed so now you have a chance to bitch at this country's horrendous airport service and swap stories about your worst delays. A side note: Unless your "worst airport delay" story involves a crash, I don't want to hear it. We've all been delayed; your story is no worse than mine.

An airport bar that strands everybody due to a violent storm or blizzard will always be my favorite. When winter weather paralyzes a city every flight is delayed, if it hasn't already been cancelled. And I don't care how many frequent flier points you've acquired or if your United frequent flier card lists you as a "Diamond, Elite, Royal, Exclusive, Entitled to Kick a Make-a-Wish recipient and his parents out of their first class seats" member, you ain't going anywhere. A snowstorm levels the playing field.

Travelers lower their guards upon realizing they are stuck and there is nothing they can do about it until the weather clears. Drinks and conversation flow freely. Cursing the elements takes a back seat. Yes, I curse in airport bars but only after seeing food and drink prices. Then again, if I ran an establishment where I knew my customers were, more or less trapped, I'd probably charge $22 for greasy quesadillas as well.

Now that I have returned to the dating world, I discovered my affinity for bars is a key component in determining commonality with potential partners. If you are ever struggling for conversation while on a date, be it a first encounter or that date which will determine whether the relationship moves forward, (for me it's always been date #3) then pose the following question:

"If you could open your own bar, and money were no object, describe it."

Note the money reference. I don't want your fantasy tavern to be void of something because you deem it too expensive. No, instead imagine a genie appeared from a bottle and made you the owner of, in your opinion, the perfect bar. Think about the décor, the food, the drink selections, the exterior, the background music, the number of televisions or lack thereof, the clientele you wish to attract and the opening and closing hours.

Once you have your answers, pose the question to your date and see how much his or her answers align with yours. eHarmony should work this way.

I posed the question to Sandra on our third "meeting." Based on her answers, if I wasn't so desiring of companionship, I would have ended the dalliance right there. It could have saved me a lot of money on wine and cheese.

Remember, Sandra was a lawyer so I could see the legal arguments and risk versus reward scenarios bouncing around her brain. Finally I reminded her there were no rules or regulations. Then the ideas flowed freely.

"I would like the theme to be modern French architecture and a heavy influence of Edith Piaf on the walls," she began.

Knowing that it's rude to google in the midst of somebody else's story, I kept my phone in my pocket, discovering later that evening that Edith Piaf was a French singer. I assumed she was an artist; why else would she be on the walls?

Sandra continued. "My wine collection would be unsurpassed, again with a heavy emphasis on French vineyards."

I also neglected to ask if Edith Piaf made her own wine.

"The menu would mostly be tapas."

Oh, so now a hint of Spain is included. Interesting but, at this point, I'd rather be watching hockey at North Star.

"And it wouldn't be cheap," she concluded. "If you're going to come to my bar, you have to be willing to pay."

Spoken like a true attorney. I'm surprised she was a criminal defense lawyer; that comment had "divorce attorney" written all over it.

Sandra continued ticking off wishes but by this time, her voice and the information she was spewing, was sounding like a flight attendant giving the preflight safety speech. I was listening to everything but absorbing nothing. The reasons? Her ideal bar was nowhere near the oasis I envisioned, one that would have a sign outside that would attract patrons from all walks of life:

DOGS DRINK FOR FREE!

That's right dog owners, I'm talking to you, which means I'm talking to about seven eighths of the world's population all of whom adopted dogs during the pandemic. OK, the figure wasn't that high but according to the American Society for the Prevention of Cruelty to Animals (ASPCA), more than 23 million American households – nearly one in five – adopted a pet during the pandemic. (ASPCA 2021) Count President Joe Biden and his German Shephard Commander among those numbers.

I don't know what percentage of those households adopted animals other than dogs but, suffice it to say, I haven't seen an army of cats, gerbils or parakeets accompanying their owners on transatlantic flights or sniffing greeting cards at the corner drugstore while their owners read and eventually chose one. It's a dog's world and we humans just live in it.

I am not sure when I became a dog lover for I grew up in a cat family. I don't even remember pleading with my parents for a dog and they weren't exactly prevalent in our neighborhood. When I played with friends who did own dogs, the pet wasn't the centerpiece of our friendship. It was just something that they owned that I did not, sort of like a treehouse or a Hot Wheels set.

Somehow I became a dog lover. When I got married, my wife brought a male Yorkshire Terrier named Barnaby into the marriage. Barnaby was about six pounds but feisty, territorial and willing to show his teeth if that territory was violated. When our first daughter arrived home he showcased his nurturing skills by jumping into the bassinet, a leap that would have made Michael Jordan proud. Yet somehow Barnaby grew on me and I shed tears when he had to be put down.

I was not averse to petting strange dogs, accompanied by their owners, on streets or in parks even though an alarming encounter with a Pitbull made me rethink my affectionate nature. I was walking one sun drenched afternoon, again in San Francisco but this time in the historic Haight-Asbury neighborhood, searching for a sports bar to watch my beloved Chicago Bears. This being San Francisco, I was soon flummoxed by the array of crisscrossed streets so common in the City by the Bay.

A male couple out walking their two Pitbulls, noticed my confusion and offered to help.

"You're really close," one said, making a "right, left, down the hill, right" motion with his hand while his partner nodded in agreement. As my eyes followed his wild gestures, I felt an excruciating pain in my kneecap. I looked down in time to see one of the pits releasing its jaws from what was now a ruined pair of blue jeans covering a blood-oozing knee.

"What the FUCK?" I yelled, loud enough to awaken the ghosts of Janis Joplin, Jimi Hendrix, Jerry Garcia and other former Haight residents.

I am not sure how one disciplines a disruptive Pitbull but I doubt it involves hauling off and smacking the dog upside the head. Which is exactly what the owner did. Embarrassed, he assured me his pooch had NEVER exhibited such behavior.

"Well…" he began.

"You're hedging," I said as I rolled up my pant leg to reveal now-clotting blood. "He has done it before, hasn't he?"

Both men looked at the sidewalk. So did the dog, who was not frothing at the mouth, snarling or desperately trying to experience what my other knee tasted like. Instead, its expression said, "Sorry but I found this talk of football boring."

The owner assured me the dog was vaccinated. He then offered to take me to his home where he said he had antiseptic and bandages.

"Great idea," I thought. "Please invite me, a stranger, into the dog's domicile. Maybe it can show me all its hiding places!"

My dog loving instincts took over. I said I wished no harm for the dog but whipped out my iPhone and demanded the owner make a statement confirming the attack in the event I needed a tetanus shot or other medical attention. The owner's demeanor immediately went from concern to "is-this-really-necessary?"

Sounding bored and put off he said, on camera, "My, uh, dog Sprout um, nipped at your knee."

"A personal injury attorney would have a field day with this guy," I thought. Where to begin? Focus on "nip" or the fact that the beast's name was "Sprout?"

Later that evening, I texted the owner asking reimbursement for my pants. Faster than it took to type this sentence, $100 appeared in my PayPal account. You can't live in Haight-Ashbury unless you have big bucks. Years later, my affection for dogs including pits, persists. I refuse to blame the dog for my injuries; instead, I blame San Francisco city planners.

Dog owners blamed me each time I recounted the story.

"What did YOU do?" seemed to be the standard response.

"I didn't do anything," I sputtered. "I was staring at my phone."

"Well, you must have done something. Dogs don't just randomly bite people. You must have provoked it."

Realizing I would never win this argument, I tried to end it with humor. "Maybe this particular breed has an aversion to Yelp," I said.

That made sense to most of my friends.

My plan for free doggy beverages took shape, ironically, as Sandra and I strolled through a neighborhood art fair one Saturday afternoon. It was one of those fairs that spring up on Chicago streets during warm weather months and create pleasant chaos as artists share the block, or in this case four blocks, with longtime retail merchants.

I saw everything from painted bamboo rods to sculptures created out of discarded auto parts to a booth sponsored by a Cadillac dealership that for reasons unknown, was allowed to hawk one of its cars in the middle of the fair. The sales representative was none too pleased when I ran my hand over the vehicle and asked if his work was titled "Cadillac on Canvas" or "Cadillac on Acrylic."

Mostly, however, I saw dogs.

I saw dogs sniffing $10,000 paintings; dogs staring at charcoal sketches, no doubt wondering if the color scheme would complement their doggy beds; heck, I saw a dog lie down in a booth and refuse to leave.

Dogs were napping beneath al fresco diners and causing pedestrian traffic jams due to their willingness to accept head scratches and belly rubs, courtesy of every art fest patron. I realized then and there that, if dogs were barred from this art festival, their owners would just as soon stay home and the term "starving artist" would apply to every painter, sculptor and jewelry maker desperately trying to make a buck in Chicago.

So I began to fantasize, if my encounters with bar patrons didn't lead anywhere, perhaps I should open my own bar and let those patrons come to me. Here is my business plan, narrated for whoever cares to listen.:

Hello dog owners, come into Pup & Sup. I am your gracious 61-year-old recently divorced proprietor. It will be my honor to serve both you and your pooch in a dark, inviting, cat-free watering hole. Now pull up a stool and order whatever you like. Your cares and troubles are already melting away, specifically because you didn't have to leave your dog behind. Order a shot for yourself and I'll pour a second, complimentary shot into one of the community dog bowls hanging behind the bar. Top shelf liquor may be exempt; even though expenses are not a prerequisite to how I run my bar, I don't think dogs care if they are drinking Old Rip Van Winkle bourbon or whatever was on sale at Wal-Mart.

Are you an IPA lover? No doubt your dog is too, as he or she has probably slurped up remnants of a beer you spilled in your own house. I will expertly tilt the dog bowl as I place it under the tap. Why should your loyal companion wait for foam to dissipate before taking that first sip?

Shortly I will give you a tour of your surroundings. Remember, this is MY fantasy bar so I have included every amenity that I would want if I were a paying customer. But first, let's go over the rules. Make sure your dog is listening because most of these guidelines apply to it. Remember, free alcohol is a privilege.

NO BARKING ALLOWED. If your dog makes a sound, even if that sound could be interpreted as "Bartender, may I please have another Budweiser" both of you will be asked to leave. That means your dog had better be chill around other dogs who may be lying under neighboring stools.

On that note, NO WANDERING. Your dog will enter my bar, lie under your stool and remain there for the duration of your visit. If you choose to shoot pool, throw darts, or even visit the restroom, your dog does not get to accompany you. This ain't an art fair!

TIP GENEROUSLY. I know your dog doesn't carry cash but you, the owner, does. For the privilege of letting your best friend into my establishment, you will leave a gratuity on the bar when you leave. I also accept Venmo.

Finally, NO OVERSERVING. If your dog can't pace itself and elects to inhale an entire drink in one slurp, it will have to wait until you order another. I will also decide when the both of you have had enough. If that happens, you will be escorted from the bar to an awaiting Uber. I'm not sure what Uber's policy is regarding dogs, but that's not my problem.

If you can abide by all these rules, let's continue the tour. Wait, your dog stays where it is…under the stool. You almost violated the NO WANDERING rule.

Do you like that framed picture of Cubs first baseman Anthony Rizzo catching the final out of the 2016 World Series? So do I. Which is why it's the first thing you see when you enter. Even the most die-hard Cubs hater can't help but smile at that photo.

That smile may be short lived as you read the NO WI-FI sign directly above Rizzo's joyous face. You are not here to write that long simmering novel or study for college finals. There's a Starbucks down the street for that. You are here to converse with fellow patrons and realize how joyful conversation can be.

No need to whip out your phone and scan some random QR code to see the beer list. It's on PRINTED *menus that you can read three inches from your face if you desire. I also won't make you squint at a chalkboard to see the selections. I'm 61; my eyesight won't even allow me, the owner, to read something like that.*

I will have 18 beers on tap, no more and no less. Six will be your run of the mill domestic choices like Budweiser and Miller Lite. The remaining dozen will be microbrews with some of the most creative titles in the beer world. I know you won't like the taste of every beer on this list but you will enjoy ordering them. May I recommend a pint of "Ungrateful Bitch?" It has sort of a biting, condescending taste but it grows on you after a while. If that doesn't please your palate, here's a sample of "Newly Single." It's a lot lighter. But it costs more. Go figure.

Are you hungry? Help yourself to what I consider to be the ULTIMATE *bar snack:* UNSHELLED PEANUTS. *Take as many as you want but no tossing the empty remnants on the floor. I know, you've been in bars where this is perfectly acceptable but I'm guessing those bars don't have dogs lying on the floor. I'm saving you a ton of money in potential veterinary bills by making sure your faithful companion doesn't leave the bar with a stomach full of salt and shells.*

My bar is void of music delivered via Pandora or Spotify playlists. You, the patron, will choose the tunes and you will do so via that jukebox stuffed with CDs at the bar's rear. Yes, you will need quarters or dollar bills to make it function. If you are under 30, find an older patron to teach you how a jukebox operates. For that matter, ask what a quarter is. Maybe you'll strike up a conversation about your divergent musical tastes but end up appreciating both Bob Dylan and Fall Out Boy.

Now please return to your stools. Bend down and give your pooch a head scratch. Can I get you both another?

Act III
THE FUTURE

"I will always try to be happy. I don't think people really understand the value of happiness until they know what it's like to be in that very, very dark place. It's not romantic. Not even a little."

–Sarah Silverman (Silverman 2010, 155)

M) When it's Cancer, Farting in Bed is Perfectly Normal

On January 24, 2024, the phone call came as I was putting the finishing touches on a contract for a homebuilding client who asked me to be their opening speaker in Las Vegas. Simultaneously, I was negotiating for a headline appearance at Zanies, Chicago's oldest and most esteemed comedy club. A VERY good day by comedian's standards.

"You have a malignant neoplasm of your ascending colon," my gastroenterologist said. "This isn't pre-cancer. It's definitely cancer."

That's a worse ending to a sentence than "…and then COVID hit."

Detected early. Very treatable. But still cancer. Of the colon. I had a car in my building's garage with a dead battery due to Chicago's frigid winter. I still wasn't divorced. Now I had cancer.

Other than that, how was the play Mrs. Lincoln?

The news wasn't entirely unexpected. In October 2023 during my 10-year colonoscopy procedure, my gastroenterologist noticed a small, irregular looking polyp His partner stepped in for the follow up and had prepped me for what his procedure would most likely confirm.

Credit the never-ending stream of back-and-forth communication between two divorce attorneys and a judge for the discovery. A year prior, when my wife and I decided to part company, I figured I had better take advantage of her health insurance for whatever ailed me, even excessive earwax. I assumed I would be divorced and on my own, insurance wise, in a few months. May as well get the Tesla treatment – a full-blown colonoscopy, performed by somebody who has seen more assholes than exist in Congress – while somebody else was paying for it.

My gastroenterologist, booked solid until the end of the calendar year, suggested the Hyundai treatment.

A home colon cancer screening test, aka "Poop in a Bag."

I waited until December 26, hoping there would be a cancellation and I wouldn't have to squat over a plastic bag and produce a fecal sample that I would gift wrap, take to the nearest UPS facility and praise the Lord that I did not choose a profession that involved opening the contents. That job sounded worse than Amazon sortation center employee.

Prior to receiving the cancer news, I had been wrestling with stories of how life can take unexpected twists and turns, often with less than desirable results. I was still reeling from news coming out of Hyderabad, India pertaining to Sanjay Shah, the 56-year-old CEO of Chicago-based Vistex Software. During a company celebration marking Vistex's 25-year anniversary, Shah and company president Raju Datla climbed into a faux hot air balloon supported by a cable. The intent was for the two to be hoisted into the air and then lowered onto the stage to begin the celebration.

I'd witnessed numerous "reveals" like this before; CEOs entering on motorcycles through clouds of steam, or piloting new automobiles the audience would soon be selling; CEOs strapped into harnesses and "juggled' onstage, courtesy of my friends from The Passing Zone; CEOs basically doing whatever it takes to appear normal and fun among the employees whose paychecks they sign.

Shah's entrance was anything but normal.

The cable gave way, plunging Shah and Datla to the stage, 20 feet below. Shah died from the fall while Datla suffered a severe head injury. The story shook me because, nine years prior, I had sat in Shah's office after he'd hired me to speak for his U.S. workforce. Despite his millions – Shah was the original owner of the Trump International Hotel & Tower penthouse in Chicago – and his reputation as a tech titan, he was beyond excited about the idea of including humor in the upcoming event. I even bounced some potential material off him, having spent a few hours perusing the Vistex website prior to the meeting.

"You just put out a press release stating you'd made some 'significant' company appointments," I told Shah. "Does Vistex ever make any 'trivial' appointments?"

Shah howled.

Now he was dead.

I recounted this story to my college friend Mark, who responded by emailing me the story of a twin-engine plane that crashed in Mooresville, North Carolina on

New Year's Eve 2023. The plane's sole occupant, pilot Randy Mysliviec, died instantly.

Mysliviec had recently sold a consulting firm for millions. He was also Mark's former boss at Convergys.

"He had everything money could buy," Mark wrote. "Life had different plans."

I wondered what life had in store for me as I entered the medical building to meet for the first time, my colorectal surgeon, Dr. Felipe Gracias. But, as in any medical appointment, vital signs and interrogation about medical history were performed by a nurse. Kathy seemed excited about my blood pressure, didn't seem concerned when I said I never smoked tobacco but had ingested other smoke forms into my lungs over the years, and pronounced me ready to meet Dr. Gracias.

"Best of luck to you," she said as she exited the room.

I realized then the seriousness of my situation, as I couldn't recall any medical professional wishing me luck when I sought help for the sniffles, plantar fasciitis, COVID, tendinitis, an impacted molar, a torn retina or numerous other maladies that accompany a 61-year-old life. I wondered if that was standard procedure in an office where every patient was carrying something inside that desperately needed to be removed? Or did she know something ominous about my particular case?

"Thanks," I said, not really knowing how to respond.

Five minutes later, Dr. Gracias appeared. I liked the guy immediately, probably because he was running 15 minutes EARLY. There are three things we have all grown accustomed to waiting for in our lives: Flights, tax refund checks and physicians. I have friends who, if you believe their stories, have doctors that allow cancer to advance from stage one to stage three before entering the room.

Dr. Gracias was a bespectacled and gregarious individual, appearing nothing like a guy who would soon be charged with inserting a camera into a hole I've always considered to be "exit only." He gave me a firm handshake, pulled up a stool (not that kind) and greeted me with a line from the "Kathy School of Patient Communication."

"I'm sorry you're here."

That was worse than "Good luck to you."

"Are you ever happy to see anyone?" I asked.

Gracias laughed and I briefly flashed back to my encounter with Shah. When a powerful person exhibits a sense of humor with a comedian, it's equally disarming for both parties. I've always believed humor is a great introductory tool as well as a tension diffuser. My dad, a lifelong salesman, was always on the prowl for one liners he could spring on potential customers. Years ago, I read an interview with famed comedian Chris Rock who recounted growing up in a tough section of Brooklyn and realized early on that survival either meant being good with your fists or your wit. If I ever wind up in prison, my initial question to the warden will be "Does this place have an open mic night?"

Anything to avoid being shanked.

I vowed to keep the mood light whenever possible. I wasn't about to turn our encounter into a comedy routine although I had already started, in my electronic file of material, a folder labeled "Colon cancer."

FIRST ENTRY: *I don't plan to talk publicly about colon cancer. Only because the words 'rectum' and 'anus' should never be uttered around other individuals. Both just sound gross. Which is why you never hear anybody in football bleachers saying 'Could you three slide your rectums to the right a little bit? If so, we'd have room for two more anuses'.*

SECOND ENTRY: *Even if I were a physician teaching medical students about colon cancer, I* STILL *couldn't use those words. I'd say "…and then you'll insert a tube into the uh, the um…you know,* DOWN THERE, *the…just look it up. It's on page 350. Let's move on."*

THIRD ENTRY*: I would never make light of breast cancer but ladies, at least you're talking about your breasts. That means you have the undivided attention of every perverted male listening to your story. In other words, every male. We would want to know all the details. 'Show me where they made the incision. Point to it. Now rub your finger around it.'*

TAGLINE: *Even doctors realize how sacred that area is. My wife had breast cancer and I remember her first appointment. The doctor who* PERFORMED THE SURGERY *on her said 'May I please examine you?' I didn't get that level of respect. Nobody said to me "Mr Schwem, do we have permission to shove numerous objects up your ass?' Would that be agreeable to you?"*

Not sure it's going to get a laugh but the audience at Zanies would soon find out.

Our witty banter quickly turned serious as Gracias told me how he would be performing a right hemicolectomy on me. He showed me drawings of a standard colon which, I don't care how you view it, looks as if it would be delicious if placed over a grill, garnished with onions and mustard and washed down with a few steins of beer at your neighborhood Oktoberfest. My tumor was laying directly where the colon makes a 90-degree right turn. Gracias told me he would be entering my colon via my navel, leaving my "exit only" hole intact, for now anyway. Once inside, he would remove part of my colon and hopefully the tumor, which he estimated at between 2 and 3 centimeters.

"Is that big?" I asked.

"Size is immaterial," he said.

Not to guys, it's not.

"I've seen ones that are huge in size and turn out to be nothing and I've seen tiny ones that are definitely something," he said.

Small penised men, there's hope for you. Well-endowed dudes, stop being so smug in the locker room!

"I just don't want to have 'tumor envy,'" I said.

According to the American Cancer Society, colorectal cancer is the third most diagnosed cancer, the numbers being slightly higher among men. (American Cancer Society 2024) Sadly, it is also the second most common cause of cancer death for men and women combined. More than 50,000 people were expected to die in 2024 from this horrible, yet easily treatable disease if caught early.

I was determined to be among the latter part of that last sentence.

My divorce, still not final, suddenly had another component. How would the diagnosis affect settlement negotiations? My wife was a breast cancer survivor; I couldn't imagine ironing out a permanent breakup while she was undergoing weekly radiation treatments.

"I guess we'll just have to wait until after surgery. See what the prognosis is" was all my attorney could say.

Surgery was scheduled one month after my meeting with Gracias. One turbocharged colon liquid prep the night before, three hours in a surgical waiting room and two incisions later, I found myself on the oncology floor of Northwestern Medicine Palos Hospital in Palos Heights, Illinois, surrounded by moans, uncontrollable fits of coughing and cries for help from other patients.

"I shouldn't be here," I thought.

But the influx of tubes, charts, IV bags and medical personnel moving in and out of Room 4625 over the next four days told me otherwise. Grappling with divorce is very similar to dealing with a serious disease. For the divorcee, it's often-unexpected news and something that "only happens to other people." Or maybe it's something that's been building up inside one's body and will eventually rear its ugly head. Once out in the open, how does the patient respond? Anger? Depression? Hopelessness? Or a willingness to beat this insidious disease, no matter the pain or the cost.

I chose the latter; being on my wife's health insurance plan sure helped.

Exactly 24 hours after surgery, Dr. Gracias stood at the foot of my bed calmly listening to me ticking off the reasons why I should be released from the hospital in the next 30 minutes. I wasn't nauseated from the surgery; my throat wasn't sore from an intubation tube; my incisions didn't hurt; I slept well, and I was STARVING.

"You're not starving," he finally interrupted. "Do you know what a quarter of the world calls a day without food? Tuesday!"

His resident, furiously taking notes on a nearby laptop, likely charted his joke.

Gracias explained I was most likely suffering from "survivor's euphoria" a common high among surgical patients, as well as soldiers who have emerged, more or less intact, from combat. I politely disagreed with Gracias; I wasn't euphoric because I had survived. I KNEW I was going to survive, had proven so and should therefore be rewarded for my correct optimism.

Physicians worldwide have probably grown accustomed to "Dr. Google," the patient who thinks he or she knows more than someone with years of medical training. COVID, the conspiracy theories as to its origins and uninformed podcast hosts like Joe Rogan, were prime contributing factors. Gracias listened politely and then asked a question that stopped me in my tracks.

"How much gas have you passed since surgery?"

"Um…none?"

End of conversation.

Twenty-four hours later I was lying in my own shit, pressing my bedside "call" button with the fervor of an eight-year-old with a Nintendo game console. Ironically, my fecal incontinence began when I was trying to accede to Gracias' wishes and produce a hefty fart or two. My body had other ideas. Had Gracias' assistant been in the room, the laptop entry would have read "Patient prone to excessive 'sharting.'"

Still, I found humor in Gracias' orders. I thought about calling my wife and saying "Remember when you used to get upset when I farted in my sleep? If you still have feelings for me, you will apologize right now."

The divorce would have proceeded regardless.

Despite my embarrassment, God was smiling on me during my operation. Three days after removing 18 inches of colon, Gracias produced two sheets of paper from his lab coat. Sifting through the medical terminology and measurements, I quickly found the one and only sentence that mattered:

"Thirteen lymph nodes. Negative for malignancy. All regional lymph nodes negative for tumor."

"You're cured," Gracias said.

I burst into tears. My team of nurses came in shortly thereafter and, with some prompting from me, danced in front of my bed as I recorded their antics on my iPhone.

Three days and a few farts later, I returned home to the 700-square-foot condo that now doubled as a recovery room. It was a scene that was all too familiar. Over a sweltering Labor Day weekend 2023, I began experiencing flu like symptoms, not exactly a common malady in 90-degree heat when the entire city was clothed in bathing suits, if that. An initial diagnosis of bronchitis became pneumonia, and I spent two weeks alternating between shivering under blankets and waking up with those same blankets drenched in sweat. Were illness and disease byproducts of divorce? In my case, it certainly appeared so.

What I do know is that misery eventually gave way to blissfulness; defeat to victory. I survived pneumonia and I survived cancer, although the latter will be a part of my life forever. Yearly PET scans, colonoscopies and an oncologist are in my future.

But I am now among the millions who can add #cancersurvivor, #cancersucks or derivatives of both to my social media profiles. Should I choose to compete in a marathon, I can proudly wear a T-shirt proclaiming "I run for colon cancer." Or maybe I'll just pass out water cups to actual runners, hoping they choose me because of my sign or my T-shirt. I did pass out water to runners in the 2023 Chicago marathon, but my introductory line was not "Hydrate for colon cancer." Instead, I held up two cups and yelled "I have mojitos AND margaritas."

Except for the Kenyans clipping along at their eight minute a mile pace, everybody laughed.

Which is the only reaction I care to hear about this insidious disease.

FOURTH ENTRY: *I had colon cancer. It was caught early, I'm fine and that's all I'm going to say. As much as I encourage it, I'm not going to be that poster child for early detection. Everybody knows that guy. You'll be at a party and he'll just casually say, 'Steve, when was the last time you had your anus scoped? Don't put that off...it saved my life. You'll thank me later. Dan, I cannot stress this enough...check your testicles! Two fingers in the shower. You'll thank me later.' (GESTURE W FINGERS) Greg, I'll thank you now if you lower those fingers. And please stay away from the dip.*

"If you must find your own path, and you are left with no easy path, then decide to take the hard path that leads you to the life and the world that you want."

– ***Stephen Colbert*** (University of Virginia 2013)

N) Finding Happiness in Sore Feet, Scandinavian Hygge and a Dead Guy

The Axios headline begged to be clicked as I opened my browser one morning in March 2024, although it wasn't the kind of story a still-not-divorced guy living in a new location and looking at a summer calendar filled with more bicycle tours than comedy gigs, wanted to read:

"U.S. Hits New Low in World Happiness Report." (Saric 2024)

NEW low? We made it through COVID right? How could things be any sadder?

I read on.

The World Happiness poll is conducted by Gallup, a Washington DC-based analytics and advisory firm that, since 1935 has been asking every ordinary citizen except me their opinions on events and trends shaping our society. Topics have ranged from the appearance of the television – in 1949, 62 percent of Americans thought the TV would "some day" replace the radio in the home – to the 1986 Challenger explosion. Seventeen years later, Gallup concluded that 80 percent of Americans thought the space program should continue, with 55 percent of men under 50 saying they would like to participate in a future flight. (Moore 2003)

"Braggadocio for sure," I thought. I'd bet what's left in my stock portfolio following the divorce half of those men would faint at the sight of their own blood or if they saw a mouse running through the shuttle. In all seriousness, as someone who was jogging in West Palm Beach, Florida that fateful January 1986 morning, heard the news on his Sony Walkman and looked up to see the craft's Y-shaped entrails clearly visible in the brilliant blue sky and signaling disaster, I was not thinking of a career change.

With the 2024 presidential election on the horizon, Gallup was still ensconced in politics, even though polls were entirely wrong in the 2016 election when Trump bested Hillary and the 2022 midterms when the "red wave" of Republican congressional candidates never declared victory. As of this writing, Joe Biden and Donald Trump were neck and neck among Gallup participants in terms of preference but neither candidate seemed to care. Biden had probably forgotten his numbers seconds after hearing them and Trump was too busy trying to raise bail money.

More troubling than which doddering fool would lead the country was the topic of happiness. Gallup concluded that in 2024, the United States had, for the first time since the happiness issue was broached, fallen out of the top 20 spots in countries surveyed. (Gallup 2024) At 23, the only countries ranking below us among the 25 happiest countries were Mexico and Germany. The former I understand, as the country is muggy, earthquake prone and full of boisterous Americans who feel Spring Break in Cancun is representative of the entire Mexican culture. Not to mention our insistence that we can master the

Spanish language by speaking slowly and loudly to Mexican natives while inserting 'O's' at the ends of certain words.

For example: ME. AND. MY. FRAT-O. BUDS. WISH. TO. CONSUME-O. MUCH-O. TEQUILA.

Germany, on the other hand, puzzled me. Once I saw German commuters drinking beer at 7:30 a.m. while waiting for trains to take them to their places of business. I wanted to move to Germany immediately. Today, with employees still resisting a return to the office post COVID, breakroom refrigerators stocked with IPA's might be a more enticing perk than on-site health clubs.

Even more puzzling was that residents in countries experiencing severe unrest – Israel and Kuwait in particular – ranked higher than us. I was once on a Zoom call with participants from Tel Aviv who had to briefly leave the call due to air raid sirens. Even then they promised to return shortly. In Chicago, I dive under my desk, dial 911 and cower in fear for hours if I hear a balloon pop.

Yet Israel still came in fifth, with only Finland, Denmark, Iceland and Sweden ranking above, leading me to wonder how much morning beer is consumed in Scandinavia?

Afghanistan ranked dead last. No surprise there.

Other takeaways I gleaned from the report's summation included:

- Happiness in India, the world's most populous country, rises the older one gets, particularly among men. I've never been to India but can't imagine how one can be happy, long term, in a country that can best be described as "shoulder to shoulder." Hell, I get pissed when the Starbucks line is more than three people.

- In sub-Saharan Africa, happiness for the young has increased. I attribute this to advances in sunscreen.

The only reason I cared about these numbers is that since electing to get divorced in late 2022 – when we ranked 16th – I had begun questioning the meaning of happiness. I had already realized I was not happy during my marriage's late stages. But was I happy now? Would I be happy after the divorce was final? After cancer? Friends and acquaintances, many who experienced divorce, assured me true happiness would come once lawyers were out of the picture and I was free to create a new life, whatever that entailed. But what exactly was their definition?

Maybe ChatGPT would know.

ChatGPT is an artificial intelligence language model developed by OpenAI. (ChatGPT 2024) It is based on the GPT (Generative Pre-trained Transformer) architecture and designed to understand and generate human-like text based on the input it receives.

How do I know this? I asked ChatGPT of course.

By 2024, ordinary citizens seemed to have forgotten they had fully functioning brains capable of generating original thoughts; instead, everybody was turning to a computer, typing queries into search boxes and letting ChatGPT spit out the answers and, basically, do their thinking for them.

It was like owning a spell checker on steroids.

Artificial Intelligence speakers were being booked into major business conferences, gleefully telling audience members how AI could "help" them do their jobs while subtly revealing AI could easily "replace" their jobs.

"AI is either the Stairway to Heaven or the Highway to Hell" one corporate client told me.

While driving for Uber, I heard multiple passengers discuss, either with fellow riders or via phone conversations, their increasing reliance on ChatGPT to offer "answers" to everything from job changes to dating preferences. My friend Tim insisted I use ChatGPT and AI to edit this book.

I resisted, mostly due to ego, pride and a journalism degree. I'll use my own smell checker, thank you very much.

But, I thought, what could it hurt to ask ChatGPT for answers on my current life status? Maybe I had overlooked something.

Early on a summer Saturday morning, I tepidly and curiously typed the following query:

"Is it possible to find happiness after a late in life divorce and beating a deadly disease?"

Within seconds, ChatGPT produced the following answers:

"Yes, it is possible to find happiness after a late-in-life divorce and beating a deadly disease, although it can be challenging. Here are some ways to navigate these difficulties and find happiness:

1. **Emotional Healing**: Seek therapy or counseling to process the emotional impact of divorce and

illness. Support groups can also provide a sense of community and understanding.

2. **Physical Health**: Focus on recovering and maintaining physical health through appropriate medical care, nutrition and exercise. This can improve both physical and mental well-being.
3. **Social Support**: Surround yourself with supportive friends and family. Building new relationships and strengthening existing ones can provide emotional support and companionship.
4. **Pursue Interests**: Engage in hobbies and activities that bring you joy and fulfillment. This can be a great way to rediscover passions and create a sense of purpose.
5. **Mindfulness and Positivity**: Practice mindfulness, meditation or other techniques to stay present and manage stress. Fostering a positive outlook can help you navigate difficult times more effectively.
6. **Set New Goals**: Establish new goals and ambitions, no matter how small. Working towards something can provide motivation and a sense of achievement.
7. **Professional Help**: Don't hesitate to seek professional help for managing stress, anxiety or depression. Mental health professionals can offer valuable strategies and support.

Each person's journey is unique, and it may take time to adjust and find a new sense of normalcy. With resilience, support and self-care, happiness is attainable even after significant life challenges."

Using two fingers, I patted my brain after digesting the list for I had, in my opinion anyway, already accomplished all seven suggestions. To recap:

1) I had sought therapy and while the results weren't entirely successful, I remain open to more.
2) I had lost 15 pounds since the divorce. Credit good eating, an in-building health club and lengthy walks and bike rides. Oh, and cancer.
3) I'd made new friends, both male and female, young and old.
4) My gig work was proof.
5) A work in progress for sure. I still found myself getting upset, angry and overly stressed at life events I could have easily handled via deep breaths or a few minutes standing on my balcony gazing at Lake Michigan. The latter works great in warm weather months but I will need to find a stress-busting alternative in January.
6) I have been a goal setter my entire life. Why stop now?
7) See #1.

So I had just proven I could think as well as a computer. ChatGPT wasn't the answer.

Maybe TikTok would know.

Despite data showing the average TikTok user is under 21, I found myself becoming addicted to the social media juggernaut I discussed in an earlier chapter. (Dunn 2024) Sleepless nights grew even worse when against my better judgment, I grabbed my phone at 2:30 a.m. and began scrolling. Within minutes I found myself rewatching scenes from favorite movies like *The Wolf of Wall Street.* What divorced guy doesn't smirk just a little when Jonah Hill's character, Donny Azoff, answers his wife's fear of "chop" aboard a yacht destined for rough seas with "I'll chop your fucking credit card in half. How about that?" (Scorsese 2013)

I downloaded cooking videos, featuring succulent delicacies one could make in an air fryer or crock pot, two appliances I insisted on when my wife and I were divvying up kitchen items. I was not as attached to the bread maker, the "Dessert Bullet," the panini press, the ice cream churner, the omelet pan or the chocolate fountain. Suffice it to say, the Schwem family never met a kitchen gadget it couldn't find space for in the pantry. The chocolate fountain was the most insipid addition; thankfully it was a Christmas gift and not a purchase. The three-tiered heap of stainless steel and plastic tubing had a moment in the late '90s. Suddenly, every dinner party and holiday gathering featured this Willy Wonka-esque machine, that spewed dark liquid chocolate over its sides. Impressive to look at, fun to sidle up to with a plateful of strawberries, marshmallows and wafer cookies, and impossible to clean.

I discovered the TikTok Shop, the network's answer to Amazon, where I purchased a rattan loveseat and in the process, gave my credit card information to Chinese spies. I viewed but never actually tried exercise regiments that guaranteed results in five minutes per day, foreign language tutorials that promised the same thing and videos showing the view a rock star has when he or she walks out to a stadium full of 80,000 crazed fans. In one video, even Coldplay members looked amazed they had sold that many tickets.

I uploaded some of my stand-up clips and then congratulated myself on achieving "likes" from users named "bunnyfufu" and "thecrushingbadass." I watched videos of new workforce participants who, instead of being grateful for full time employment, bitched that their jobs left them with no money for daily Starbucks or new yoga mats. I saw adorable puppies being rescued from roadside ditches after being abandoned by cruel owners. I encountered crying babies who stopped crying after their parents threw cheese slices in their faces. Note to prospective parents and grandparents: DEFINITELY keep some Kraft singles in the fridge.

During one of these late-night binges, Rebecca Kordecki appeared. Kordecki is an LA-based fitness trainer and "life coach," a term I was rapidly becoming familiar with as these people, along with AI experts, were crushing it on the speaker circuit. The term "life coach" seemed so pretentious. Also, so broad. A professional baseball player is fully authorized to coach baseball; ditto for a speech coach who makes a living as a public speaker. But what qualifies a person to take another person's entire life and offer improvement tips, particularly from the passenger seat of a moving car, where Kordecki filmed most of her TikTok videos? I wondered if her driver was silently thinking "I'd be WAY happier if I could give up this job. I'd even go without the Starbucks!"

In Kordecki's case, it all came down to breathing. She's also a "breathwork" coach (yeah, that's a thing) according to her website which screams, "BECOME THE

BADASS BOSS OF YOUR HAPPY so you crush part 2 of your life!" And no, she's not the "crushingbadass" who liked my stand-up video. I checked.

Like me, Kordecki is in her 60s so I figured watching a few videos couldn't hurt. Put me in…coach!

During one TikTok video Kordecki emphasized a four-step process, repeated daily for 21 days that, in her words would make one "happier, less depressed and less anxious than if you were to take any medication for the same amount of time." (@rebeccakordecki, January 18, 2023)

Step one was breathing for two minutes a day.

The comedian in me wanted to message Kordecki and remind her that, if we only breathed daily for two minutes, we'd all be dead and she could stop making car videos. But that wasn't her point; instead, she wanted me to watch and listen to my breath for 120 seconds, free of distractions like my phone and my computer. I didn't think I could ever master *watching* my breath unless I did it in subzero temperatures, but I did subscribe to her second recommendation:

Moving your body.

Kordecki suggested a brisk walk, cycling, kayaking, or just getting outside in nature for 15 minutes. Like millions of Americans during COVID, I became an avid walker. So did former Wall Street Journal reporter Neil King, who set off from Washington, D.C. on March 29, 2021 and didn't stop walking until he arrived in New York City, 26 days later. Upon completing his journey, he tweeted "Do not be conformed to this world, but be transformed by the renewing of your mind. That simple walk transformed and renewed me." (@NKingofDC, April 24, 2021)

No doubt he wrote that while watching his breath.

I told myself I was walking to lose weight and I succeeded at dropping a few pounds. But my walks, which should have been the perfect time to rekindle a relationship with my wife, were largely done solo. I often wondered if neighbors seeing me strolling past their homes alone and lost in my own thoughts saw the writing on the wall.

Number three was "gratitude journaling" defined by Kordecki as writing down or speaking something that I was grateful for, either today, yesterday or last week. I passed on this one only because I write for a living. I know it's a lame excuse, but I figured I could speak my gratitude on those 15-minute exercise jaunts.

Finally, she suggested emailing someone in my life who has touched me. Other than immediate family who have been recipients of emails with subject lines ranging from "I'M IN LAWYER HELL!" to "I think I have early onset dementia," I decided to table that one for the time being.

However, curiosity led me to search "How to find happiness" on TikTok, just to see who else was trying to solve this riddle and boost our nation's Gallup poll numbers. I could have spent all day at my computer, so plentiful were the accounts. But that would have violated step two of Kordecki's happiness action plan and, since I had anointed her as my life coach for the time being, I thought it wise to limit my searches.

David Bederman, a "soul coach," tells his 65,000 TikTok followers to adopt a "surfer's mentality" to find happiness. (@coach_tipz, October 8, 2022) Bederman claims surfers know the perfect wave is elusive.

"The wave is going to crash and that they're going to fall and maybe another wave is going to crash on top of them," Bederman says. "But they don't let that get them down because a surfer understands that there's always more waves coming."

I live in relatively wave-free Chicago and my place isn't big enough to house a surfboard. I kept searching.

Sadly, Gallup poll data revealed that Gen Z's and millennials in the United States were markedly unhappier than their counterparts in other countries. I often lectured my girls on how their 20s should be the happiest times of their lives. Looking back, it certainly was for me. Then again, I didn't have to deal with soul crushing housing prices, a hyper charged political climate, or a global pandemic that meant spending massive hours in front of a computer, reading and watching social media posts from others in my age bracket who had managed to find beaches and nightclubs free of masks and disease. These kids are plentiful on social media; none seem to have jobs but all have passports. Yet some had apparently found happiness without jetting off to exotic destinations and were only too happy to share their secrets on TikTok. Maybe I would glean something.

First, I had to get past the props these kids were using in their videos. Fitnessbyanni listed her happiness secrets while applying a series of creams and drops to her face and adding a plug for Core Greens, a nutritional supplement from @Zahler Nutrition. (@fitnessbyanni, June 23, 2023) She had six tips for achieving happiness, the last being to minimize space and "get rid of things you don't need anymore." She revealed this while applying lip balm.

Alexx.fitt said she was genuinely happy but said so while twisting a pair of wired air buds, leading me to wonder if she was simply regurgitating advice from whatever podcast she was currently listening to. (@alexx.fitt, August 17, 2023)

Nicki_Andrea who, like Kordecki, chose a car's passenger seat to record her happiness secrets, said it was all about being "silly."

"Like I think it's genuinely taken me until my late '20s to realize that like no one actually cares and the more that you just let yourself go and have fun, the better life will be every single day." (@nicki_andrea, January 2, 2024)

Andrea (I assume that's her last name) clutched an enormous Chick-fil-A cup while recording. I messaged her and asked if beverages from the chicken franchise were part of her solution. I am still awaiting an answer.

Casey Kellyy's prop consisted of his abs. (@caseykellyy, December 18, 2023) His profile intrigued me only because I've never encountered a double "y" in the name "Kellyy." Or maybe another Casey Kelly claimed the name before Kellyy discovered TikTok. Thar's how I feel when I see a gmail address like JasonMiller6541@gmail.com. Does that mean there are 6540 other Jason Millers out there with gmail accounts?

Casey looked 18 at most but his youth didn't stop him from posting a video he titled "How To Be Truly Happy." At first view, the audio on my phone wasn't functioning properly. Without sound, it appeared Casey's goal to happiness was to skateboard, spend inordinate amounts of time in the gym lifting weights and then record himself flexing in various locations, including aboard a boat. However, when the audio corrected itself, I was able to HEAR Casey reveal the true secret to happiness, which was to skateboard, spend inordinate amounts of time in the gym lifting weights and flex aboard a boat.

Back in what appeared to be his bedroom, away from his world of barbells and nutritional supplements, Casey added this nugget: "Become really good at something you enjoy. Not only will you be doing something that makes you happy, but you'll also feel a sense of accomplishment."

His advice was not lost on his 487,000 TikTok followers, one of whom commented, "I'm going to master Fortnite. Thanks for the advice."

Fortnite, as I learned from my wife's nephews, is a video game that requires spending massive amounts of time in front of a computer.

I decided I had to find videos that didn't involve the subjects eating, slurping, contorting or beautifying themselves, as it was distracting me from their messages. Focus on the spoken narrative instead, I told myself.

Ashleyd1229 posted "Four sentences that will make you rethink your life." (@ashleyd1229, July 6, 2022) A male with a slight British accent served as narrator. But, as he ticked off each sentence, I found myself staring at the scene either he or Asheleyd had chosen to use as the backdrop. It featured a young woman sitting on street trolley tracks in a steady rain. Her long brown hair and shirt were soaked. Her knees were pulled in and she balanced her weight on her palms, resting flat on the pavement behind her posterior. It looked like somebody had just dumped her out of the trolley and she was left to contemplate how to get home. Without an umbrella. Hardly a happy situation.

I did find all four sentences relatable, some more than others:

1) Happiness is not the absence of problems. It's the ability to deal with them.
2) Feeling sad after making a decision doesn't mean it was the wrong decision.
3) You're not stressed because you're doing too much. You're stressed because you're doing too little of what makes you feel most alive.
4) The lesson you struggle with will repeat itself until you learn from it.

Was I "dealing" with my divorce? Yes, but that involved mounting legal bills, briefs spelling out who would pay for what and emails and texts that probably should never have been sent. None of that induced happy feelings.

Yes, there have been moments, even days and weeks, of sadness following our mutual decision to go our separate ways. But I have never once felt I made the wrong decision to agree to a late in life divorce, even though I made my half of the decision in a darkened parking lot after seeing a cover band. I'm not sure where my ex was when she decided to become newly single.

Like sadness, my stress level has fluctuated during this process. But I've dealt with it by doing precisely what unnamed British guy – and ChatGPT - suggested. I took on side hustles, made new friends, dated and found new interests, many of which I've recounted in this book. I've never felt more alive than I do now. Sadness has taken a back seat to adventure.

Finally, I asked myself if divorce involved learning lessons. The biggest lesson, it was fast becoming clear, was not to seek advice via social media.

Doing so is like trying to talk to someone through a room with a one-way mirror. You can hear what the person on the other side is saying but they never hear your objections. And you don't get to add your own thoughts.

Now, my thoughts turned to Al. Short for Allen, not Artificial Intelligence.

I never knew Al's exact age for the entire time we were acquainted. I only knew that he was retired, living in a nearby suburb, married and occasionally in need of airport transportation. That's how we met; he had prearranged an Uber ride one afternoon and I arrived to find him and his wife Carole waiting for me in their driveway, bound for Midway.

The 35-minute ride was cordial enough that I offered the couple my services any time they needed an airport lift, my schedule permitting. They gladly accepted and I looked forward to these rides, as the couple were always punctual, chatty and paid in cash. Conversation topics ranged from life in Chicago – I discovered the pair had lived mere blocks from my current residence before fleeing to the suburbs – to their grandson's struggles with leukemia. Occasionally, politics entered the conversation despite my best attempts to steer clear of such a divisive topic. Al was a career finance man but after retiring, had found a side hustle as an election poll worker, a job he discussed with immense pride.

While squiring them home from Midway one blustery winter day, I told them of my upcoming show at Zanies. The show was fast approaching and I was spreading the word among friends.

"That sounds like fun," Al said. Carole agreed.

They promised to bring friends of their own. They refused my offer of complimentary tickets. I sent a reminder text two weeks before the show, but it wasn't necessary as I subsequently received a list of attendees and there were four tickets under Al's name. Paid in full.

That night, when I arrived at the club, Al, Carole and another couple were already in their seats, surrounded by patrons much younger. No real surprise at their early arrival. Suburbanites venturing to the big bold city of Chicago tend to begin their journeys earlier than if they were catching flights to Australia. This is because they are convinced traffic will be bumper to bumper the minute they leave their driveways, there will be zero parking spaces available within five-mile radiuses of their destinations and, if they arrive past sundown, it greatly increases their chances of being murdered.

It had been a while since I'd headlined a comedy club having elected to spend the last 25 years chasing corporate gigs and sailing around the world. I found I missed seeing audience members on ancient wooden chairs, balancing drinks on equally ancient cocktail tables as waitresses adeptly moved through the room, taking orders while not disturbing my act. As soon as I hit the stage the laughs rained down, making me the happiest person in the room, for 45 minutes anyway. If a Gallup poll worker had interviewed me mid-show, our country's ranking would have risen a notch or two simply based on my answers. I also would have suggested Casey Kellyy put down the barbells and hit an open mic night.

After the show, I found Al as he and his party prepared to leave.

"Great show," he said. "I haven't laughed that hard in a very long time."

I never saw Al again.

Three days after the show, I received an email from Carrie, one half of the couple who had accompanied Al and his wife.

"Greg, it was so nice meeting you and we really enjoyed the show on Monday" it began.

Then, "I have sad news. Al passed away Monday evening. He seemed fine driving home and we all had a great time."

Al died in his sleep.

Stunned, my mind kept racing back to that final handshake in the club. It occurred after his final meal, his final "date night" and just prior to his final car ride. So many finalities.

But then I realized something that no poll could conclude. Al died happy. At least I choose to think he did.

He spent his last night on earth with the love of his life and friends surrounding him. He belly laughed. For 90 minutes – consisting of my set and the two comics who proceeded me – his grandson's health, his own aches and pains (I assume he had some for, when I read his obituary, I learned he was 72) and the 2024 election no longer troubled him.

Everybody should go out that way.

Yet Al was dead. I was still very much alive. Which is why I decided I needed to explore the happiness question further via people in the prime of their lives as opposed to those like me who were approaching their sunset years. I wanted to talk to a generation that had yet to experience issues like marriage, kids, relocation, divorce, illness and more of life's speedbumps. What had they learned from earlier generations? Did they have plans for achieving happiness? Were they acting on them? If I could see how that generation lived perhaps I could mimic some of their actions, even though I wasn't interested in living entirely like a 20-something. Going to bed at 4:30 a.m., my normal wake up time, didn't seem feasible at my age.

Surrounded by this age group, observing their movements, and eavesdropping on their conversations fascinated me. I wear earbuds when I'm in the gym but shun them on walks or whenever I'm in public places, preferring to listen to idle chatter and the chance to jump into conversations and learn about people in the process.

What intrigued me the most was the way this generation valued experiences over money; the way they leaped from job to job, not caring that their resumes were starting to look like novels; their preference for dogs over children, for non-alcoholic beverages over the real stuff. While driving for Uber, a passenger who worked for a major liquor distributor informed me that 25 percent of adults under 25 shunned alcohol. A second passenger, who I picked up a month later and also worked in the liquor business, confirmed those numbers.

I asked the obvious. "What ARE they drinking?"

"CBD infused beverages."

I tried one shortly thereafter but didn't get quite the buzz I was hoping for, considering it was ten bucks for a four-pack. Though it did make me considerably happier.

Finding subjects in this age group to interview netted mixed results. I chose, as my interrogation room, F.O. Mahoney's. Nestled on the edge of Chicago's gay neighborhood, the corner tavern quickly became my bar of choice, not only for its proximity to my condo, but its personality which seemed to change each time I entered. During my first visit, I assumed it was a gay bar as evidenced by the all-male clientele knocking back beers, the scantily dressed male bartender and, as mentioned, its location. However, a few male/female couples were seated on the establishment's outdoor patio enjoying the Spring warmth. I drank one beer and left but vowed to return, still not convinced of the establishment's personality.

During my second visit, I walked into what appeared to be a full throttled sports bar. Numerous baseball and soccer games were on the bar's TVs, watched, with varying degrees of interest, by men and women ranging in age from 25 to 65. I struck up a few conversations and got a few phone numbers, but not in hopes of romantic trysts. I was merely looking for interview subjects.

Some didn't see it that way.

Keenan was 23 and entrenched in his first post-college job at an e-commerce marketplace. Sitting alone at Mahoney's, he was actively watching the NBA draft selection, waiting for his beloved Portland Trail Blazers to announce a pick and agonizing over who that pick might be.

"If it's Zach Edey, I'm going to kill myself. Really," he said in between mouthfuls of something called a Wrigley Burger, which contained peanut butter.

I was tempted to tell him that if a college draft announcement made him contemplate suicide, maybe it was best to stay single forever. Or always live in ground-floor units.

The Blazers chose Donovan Clingan. Crisis averted, we resumed our conversation. I marveled at his communication abilities, his interest in people other than himself and the ease at which he recounted the problems he was having with his current girlfriend. I briefly mentioned the book I was writing and asked for his number. He obliged, we left together and went our separate ways.

Four days later I texted, asking him if he'd like to sit for an actual interview.

Crickets.

Maybe he thought I was hitting on him. I'd only touched him once, putting a hand on his shoulder and saying "I got your back" when the Blazers prepared to make their pick. But I've already recounted what can happen in bars when my hands wander, no matter the intent.

Nick and Danyelle were happy to help.

I met Nick, 28 at the time, during the third trip to Mahoney's. I had just returned from a Cubs day game with a friend who had evening plans. Not wanting to call it a night at 5:15 p.m., I grabbed a stool, ordered a beer and noticed Nick sitting by himself two stools over, his focus shifting between the television and his phone.

I don't recall the icebreaker that started our conversation but, within minutes, we were amiably chatting. I learned he was from Wisconsin, had attended Vanderbilt University and moved to Chicago to begin a career as an accountant for a well-known liquor brand. What was it with me and liquor business employees?

Like Keenan, I complimented him on his gift for conversation – a skill I feel so many 20-somethings lack due to their phones. President Barack Obama alluded to this in the speech he delivered at the 2024 Democratic National Convention.

"We live in a time of such confusion and rancor, with a culture that puts a premium on things that don't last – money, fame, status, likes. We chase the approval of strangers on our phones; we build all manner of walls and fences around ourselves and then wonder why we feel so alone. We don't trust each other as much because we don't take the time to know each other." (Roush 2024)

I also told Nick I appreciated the fact that he didn't think I was hitting on him. No reason for another Keenan episode.

Nick revealed he was in a long-distance relationship, his girlfriend still at Vanderbilt but planning a move to Chicago in a few months. They would cohabitate. Despite our age differences, Nick and I seemed to have plenty in common, namely strangers in a big city and looking for friends, or at least conversation. We exchanged numbers but I didn't think I would see him again. I was 32 years his senior; who hangs out, socially, with someone old enough to be their father?

Nick for one.

During our third meeting, I met Danyelle. By now she had secured a job in HR and the move to Chicago was imminent. During future encounters they would accept my invitations to Mahoney's, or vice versa, but would also spread the word to their friends, unbeknownst to me. A table for three suddenly turned into a table of seven or eight. At first, I assumed I was the reason. Maybe Danyelle thought, erroneously, I had eyes for her boyfriend and she didn't need competition. But I quickly realized these two were friendly, social Gen Z's who, like me, saw Mahoney's as the perfect gathering spot for camaraderie. Never once did I catch any of their friends warily eyeing me, their expressions saying "Who's the creepy old guy?" Like Nick and Danyelle, they were chatty, personable and more than willing to share tidbits about their lives.

One of their male friends entertained me with a story of his evening plans which consisted of attending, solo, a concert at the Byline Bank Aragon Ballroom on Chicago's North Side. I don't recall the artist's name but I will never forget his musical genre.

"He's a well-known mumble rapper," the friend said.

"Excuse me. What?"

"MUMBLE rapper."

"Don't all rappers mumble?" I asked. I mean, I'm still trying to decipher the lyrics to M.C. Hammer's 'U Can't Touch This" and that's been a 30-year project.

"So this guy just mumbles on stage and you pay for that?" I continued, chuckling at my own words so the friend wouldn't think I was being judgmental.

He laughed too before adding, "It's more than that."

Wikipedia defines "mumble rap" as "mumbling or unclear vocal delivery by artists and has been used to describe rappers who do not share the genre's traditional emphasis on meaningful lyricism, choosing instead to emphasize other aspects of delivery like vibe, melody, and tone." (Iandoli 2016)

I applauded him on his decision to attend the concert alone. I never would have considered such a thing in my 20s.

Eventually, I revealed to Nick and Danyelle that I was writing a book about my search for late in life happiness. I asked if they'd be willing to answer a few questions about that topic. Both immediately agreed.

Naturally, the meeting took place at Mahoney's on a Sunday afternoon. By now we'd grown very comfortable around one another. The pair knew of my cancer treatment and my ongoing divorce issues. They'd even attended one of my stand-up shows.

Both walked into the bar moving very slowly. Neither pushed back when I asked if they were hung over. Nick ordered a beer while Danyelle nursed her maladies with ginger ale.

"Are you happy today?" I asked them both.

"I'm not happy that I have to work tomorrow," Danyelle replied. "The hangover doesn't help. But it's sunny outside."

Nick chose to ruminate on happiness in the future, not the present.

"I never want to lose community. Or be lonely," he said. "I want to be able to pay my bills and, once in a while, go on a nice trip to somewhere new. I want to become smarter and never be a grumpy old man."

"We definitely agree on the last part of that sentence," I said.

I dove deeper into their pasts and their relationship. They met at a New Year's Day party in Tennessee where Danyelle labeled Nick "boring." Obviously, her feelings changed.

They've discussed marriage but want to "date" one another for at least another year. They've explored Paris together and talked about raising a family but, like so many couples I've met of their generation, seemed to hedge when realizing how offspring could upend their lifestyles.

"Since moving here, I thought, 'Maybe I'd be OK just being the fun aunt,'" Danyelle said.

Her words seemed to weigh heavily on her, having been a nanny for 14 years. She even broached the "having kids" subject with Nick early in their courtship.

"We were driving to dinner, and I said 'I need to know something. Do you see yourself wanting kids?' And he said 'I don't know'" she recalled.

Nick looked sheepish while Danyelle continued. "I said 'I need you to reflect on that because, if you don't, that's a deal breaker.'"

"We are definitely getting a dog," Nick said, lightening the mood.

Shocker!

The conversation took a darker turn. Danyelle's parents were divorcing after 30 years of marriage. I asked if she'd ever heard the term "Gray Divorce." She hadn't.

She admitted to being on anti-depressants and was currently in therapy. Nick also had briefly sought counseling, feeling overwhelmed by a job that at the time, involved 70-hour work weeks while his potential wife was 300 miles away. Both questioned if they would ever be truly happy. For Nick, it was the dream of someday owning a home, be it one filled with kids, dogs or both.

"Rents just keep going up and we feel like we are never going to be able to afford a house," he said.

"So home ownership is the main factor that's making you unhappy?" I asked.

"Well, that and climate change," he said.

Danyelle, whose medication helped her cope with bouts of unhappiness, had been wrestling with the issue of women's rights since the Supreme Court overturned Roe vs. Wade two years earlier.

"I don't know if I could bring a child into this world and then not let them have rights over their own bodies," she said, in between ginger ale sips.

Both said they would vote Democratic in 2024, primarily due to the party's support for upholding a woman's right to choose.

"I have a good, comfortable life," Danyelle added. "I can afford almost everything I need and I have good friends. Could it be better? Sure. Happiness is a momentary thing. Some people try to live their lives under an umbrella of happiness. I don't think that's possible."

"But you're happy today?" I asked again, wondering if their feelings had changed after such heavy conversation.

The pair looked at one another, as if to say "You answer that." I realized, as I had begun suspecting, that happiness has no definition despite what anyone, TikTokkers included, believes.

I returned to my smallish, rented condominium. I opened a cabinet and watched Tupperware containers spill out. I lamented the fact that, at 61, I was living in a space that didn't have room for Tupperware.

I checked my stock portfolio, knowing the amount was not enough to retire on. I checked my eerily empty work calendar knowing my nest egg wouldn't rise unless prospective clients started calling. I began feeling as far from the happiness spectrum as one could be.

A month later, an opportunity fell from the sky or, more specifically, rolled in from the ocean. My cruise ship agent emailed and said a comedian had to cancel a date aboard the Celebrity Apex. Would I like to fill in for a week? I checked the itinerary, which Celebrity had entitled "Best of Scandinavia" and saw the first two stops were Copenhagen, Denmark and Helsinki, Finland.

Major cities in the world's two happiest countries in the world according to the Happiness Report.

What an opportunity! I would meet Danes and Finns in person, as opposed to seeing photos of them in the Happiness Report, their smiling mugs accompanying happiness charts and graphs. It was like finding the answers to a final exam, hours before actually taking it.

I eagerly accepted, flew to Southhampton, England two weeks later and boarded the Apex. Upon arrival in Copenhagen, I logged onto TripAdvisor searching for a tour. Many of my Bobby's Bike Hike customers found their tours using the same method so I figured it was better than wandering the streets of an unfamiliar city before getting run over by a bicycle.

Ah yes, the bicycle. In Copenhagen, this two-wheeled transportation mode may as well be the city symbol, bird, flower, whatever. Everybody owns one and everybody uses it to get everywhere. It's not uncommon to see HUNDREDS of bikes outside public establishments, identical looking to me but not to the owners, who can locate their bikes faster than I could find my car in a lot with eight parking spaces.

TripAdvisor offered several tours, some on foot and some on bikes. One caught my eye:

"Good Morning Copenhagen: Feel the Danish Hygge & Happiness."

I remember seeing "hygge," pronounced "Hue-ga," on a sweatshirt somewhere but thought nothing of it. Now before spending 68 bucks to learn its definition, I googled it and discovered it was "a defining characteristic of Danish culture; a quality of coziness and comfortable conviviality that engenders a feeling of contentment or well-being." (Buder 2023)

That was enough for me. The next morning, I took a bus from the cruise ship to the Copenhagen city center and then set off on foot for the 20-minute journey to the tour's starting point. Hundreds of bicycles, some of their occupants wearing suits or expensive skirts, whizzed past me. Very few wore helmets. I hoped I would not have to stop any of them and ask if I was correctly heading to the intersection between Øster Voldgade and Kronprinsessegade.

Miraculously, Google Maps got me there. Two minutes later Jacob, the tour guide appeared. Eight other participants, all American, followed shortly thereafter. Unlike the Rome tour, there were a few solo travelers on this one including Mark, retired and living in Santa Rosa, California. He was the first to arrive after me and we discovered we had both grown up in the same Illinois suburb of Arlington Heights.

A weird coincidence for sure.

Jacob introduced himself as 38, of Sri Lankan descent and still not sure what he wanted to do with his life, despite a marketing degree and training as a pastry chef. Unlike me who gave tours as a side hustle, squiring Americans around the streets of Copenhagen was his full-time gig.

He spoke seven languages and said he knew "a little" Italian and Japanese but was not yet comfortable conversing in either. I neglected to speak Spanish with him.

"I'M FROM A CRUISE-O SHIP-O!"

We began the tour and quickly found ourselves on Krusemyntegade, also known as Mint Street. Even Jacob seemed relieved he could shorten the pronunciation.

Lined with multi-colored row house, street lamps and rose bushes, Jacob revealed it was his favorite stopping point. Why? Because it produced, in his opinion anyway, the most hygge.

I whipped out my iPhone and recorded his explanation.

At first it sounded like he was repeating the Google definition, using words like "comfort," "contentment" and "conviviality." But then his personal thoughts took over.

"Hygge is any given situation, in which you find yourself, where you are surrounded by a lack of annoyances," he said. "It is a state of mind more than it is a materialistic thing. It is very abstract and subjective, and people have their own ideas as to what it means to them."

Krusemyntegade Street, he continued, could be described as "quaint," "charming" or "picturesque" yet Danes would simply call it a very "hygge-ly" street.

Having already used hygge as a noun and adjective, Jacob said it could also be a verb, i.e. "Let's hygge in the park today." But, he cautioned, if one accepts an invitation to hygge, don't bring along material possessions, particularly your phone.

I stopped recording.

"Enjoy each other's company and try to be present with other people, not just physically but also mentally. Engage and interact."

As the tour continued, I realized that in this country of 6 million bike-crazed residents, even the youngest residents embraced hygge. We encountered numerous Danish school groups and field trips touring the city's beautiful parks, churches and castles where Danish kings have resided since 1513. All have been named, alternatively, Frederik and Christian, two very un-hygge-ly names in my opinion but who am I to question royal tradition? What I did learn is that Denmark's current king, Frederik X, will eventually be succeeded by his son, Crown Prince Christian. If he squires a son, that heir must be named Frederik. If he produces a daughter, the future queen, she will be called Margrethe.

What struck me about the groups, even those consisting of pre-teens and teenagers, is that not one participant carried a cell phone. All were, as Jacob described, in the moment, physically and mentally. Conversation flowed freely.

In his 2017 book, *The Little Book of Hygge,* Meik Wiking breaks hygge into five dimensions. Wiking, incidentally, is the CEO of the Happiness Research Institute, Copenhagen and I doubt one ascends to that position without knowing a thing or two about hygge. I wonder if he ever has a bad day?

Hygge, Wiking explains, could be a taste. "If you want your stew to be more hyggelig, you add wine," he writes. (Wiking, 2017, 197) It could also be sounds such as crackling fireplace wood or rain on rooftops, smells from your past, touching hygg-ly things such as a warm ceramic cup, or observing slow-moving scenes like gently falling snow. A sixth component, he said, is feeling safe. That means trusting where you are and who you are with.

Jacob found Denmark so hygge-ly compared to other countries he'd lived in, Japan and the United States included, that he had no plans to leave. Our tour concluded with the nine of us sitting with Jacob at an outdoor café, conversing about random topics. Our group consisted of a cardiologist, a pharma rep, a real estate agent, a school teacher, an IT administrator, a comedian and three retirees. Only the real estate agent kept stepping away to exhibit very un-hygge-ly behavior, courtesy of her phone. The rest of us were content. And happy.

I could have stayed in the café all day, eventually swapping cappuccino for wine and talking until the sun set which, in Scandinavia during summer months, occurs around midnight. But the ship was leaving and I had to get back. I wished Jacob and the group well, returned to the Apex and spent the rest of the evening hygge-ling with fellow cruisers at one of the ship's many bars.

Helsinki, Finland beckoned.

Forty-four hours later the rumble of anchors and the slight sway in my cabin meant we had docked in the world's happiest country. I had two performances that evening and, on show days, I try to limit my sightseeing, as disappointing as that may be. When I need a game plan, as opposed to just wandering in a strange country or city and seeing what transpires, I turn to Mike, a fellow comedian and travel podcast host. Mike has worked ships for more than 20 years and has seemingly visited every country containing a body of water big enough to handle a cruise ship's draft. Never married, I admired his willingness to explore our planet on his own.

Six months after separating, sitting (solo naturally) at an outdoor restaurant in Ravetta, Malta, I texted him. "Do you ever get tired of traveling alone?"

"Of course," he texted back. "But I prefer it to being with someone who doesn't want to be there. I don't compromise well when it's somewhere I really want to go. That would explain being single all these years I guess."

Now, intrigued with finding the world's happiest people in the world's happiest country, I asked for suggestions in Helsinki.

"Do as a local and sit naked in a sauna with strangers," he said.

That might make me happy, depending on my sauna mates. Not sure the reverse would be true, considering they would have to stare at my aging body which now included a cancer surgery scar.

Finland's 5.4 million population boasts more than 3 million public and private saunas. Men and women sweat in saunas; women give birth in saunas; politicians have been known to solve problems by sitting naked with one another until solutions are reached and treaties ironed out. It's called "sauna diplomacy." Then vice-president George W Bush reportedly jumped naked into the Baltic Sea after a sauna session with his Finnish counterparts in 1983.

Note: Author had to briefly put head between knees and breathe deeply after envisioning Donald Trump or Joe Biden engaging in sauna diplomacy.

So how could this country, that gets 20 hours of daylight in summer but less than six in winter, and shivers through three months of subzero temperatures, be dubbed the world's happiest country? I vowed to find out, with or without clothes.

Grabbing a bathing suit in case I ended up in a co-ed sauna, I set my sites on Villi Waino, a two mile walk from the ship. I was already perspiring when I arrived, only to be told reservations required a group of at least six, with prices for a three-hour sauna starting at 300 euros or about $320. That seemed pricey for an orgy, not that I had any experience in that sort of thing.

I had passed Loyly shortly after getting off or "disembarking" as we cruise veterans like to say but kept walking fearing it would be inundated with passengers from the States. I wished for a more authentic experience. But with time slipping away, I decided Loyly might be my only choice. Reversing direction, I headed back, entered and found the place to be alive with sauna patrons milling about in robes, bathing suits and rubber sandals. None were naked although there were a few Scandinavian women who I wished had forgotten their suits.

Armed with a towel and a small cloth to sit on, I started in the stone sauna, the hottest of the four at 190 degrees. No, that's not a misprint. I was alone for only a few minutes when a woman in a thong bikini and an ample set of breasts entered, sitting mere feet away. I adjusted my towel, until this moment covering my knees and ankles, ever so slightly.

Samantha, or "Sam" as she preferred, was a college student from Colorado who had come to the happiest country on earth to study…wait for it…Finnish crime. I asked if she'd read the Gallup poll and whether she planned to turn in a one-page thesis that read simply "There is none."

"All countries have crime," Sam corrected me. "It's just not as out in the open as in America."

I pressed Sam for details but she seemed hesitant to reveal her findings. Eventually I gave up, turning the discussion to why we were still sitting in this microwave oven and was it doing anything for our moods? Personally, it's hard to feel happy when your skin is bubbling and your Apple Watch, which you should have left in the locker room, is melting.

"I'm ready to jump in the water," she said. "How about you?"

"The water" was where Bush had made his mark while vice president. The Baltic Sea lay just outside the sauna, calm, picturesque and 59 degrees. A single ladder meant occupants had to enter one at a time. Trust me, nobody JUMPS into the Baltic.

Gingerly, Sam entered the water letting it creep up to her neck before pronouncing herself done and climbing out.

"Your turn," she said.

I gripped the ladder's sides, descended a few steps until my feet and knees met the surface, dunked my butt into the frigid conditions and began ascending.

"All the way," Sam said. "To your neck. You can't come all the way to Finland and just get your feet wet. Get back in there."

I laughed and did as instructed. I climbed out with a huge smile on my face, not because I had conquered polar temperatures but because this chance interaction, with a person a third my age, was causing happiness. Shrinkage too but genuine happiness.

Sam left soon after but I still had a good hour left on my 35-dollar session, enough time to enter a second sauna with a glass wall, allowing its occupants to gaze at the Baltic while perspiring. I sat between a 20-something American and a woman about the same age, not realizing they'd been having a conversation prior to my entrance and I was now the object that had come between them. I took the hint and left.

I wandered back inside towards the locker room where I saw a closed door labeled "Open to Public." Opening the door, I saw six occupants: a young Asian couple, two American men about my age and Sarah, 36 and a native Finn. I asked her if she and her country people were truly as happy as the Gallup poll suggested.

"Yes," she replied, somewhat haltingly. "But I think that's due to our welfare system."

Long praised for a system that seeks to eliminate class structure, Finns of all income levels enjoy ample vacation time, maternity leave and free public healthcare. I don't know the first question a Finnish doctor hears when he's about to set a broken leg but it definitely isn't "What's this gonna cost?"

So was my key to happiness abandoning my cell phone as they seem to have done in Denmark? I mean, how would my lawyer get hold of me, reminding me that I still owed him money? Or as Wiking suggests, maybe I should smell my childhood blanket. Or add copious amounts of cooking sherry to my next meal, even if that meal came from HelloFresh meal delivery service. But I kept coming back to Steve Martin's dream, revealed in Chapter One. Like him, my personal happiness, or hygge, was people. People, not phones and robots, are the best communicators and, therefore, the best happiness providers, for happiness is about opening up, expressing your feelings, telling your stories and having an inquisitive mind and sympathetic ear for those willing to do the same. As my Uber profile stated "Everybody has a story. What's yours?"

I am grateful for all the friends and strangers who lent me their minds and ears. Whether it was the random cruise ship passenger, the fellow cancer survivor, the airport bar patron or anybody else who entered my life during its most difficult phase, all I can say is "thank you." For listening. For offering advice when you, or I, thought it was warranted. I haven't always taken that advice but it's great to hear a fresh perspective. Or ideas.

As I complete this book I am repeatedly checking my watch, as I have to catch a train to the suburbs. Today I will be undergoing some dental work, followed by a visit with my accountant. Two very "un-hyggly" moments for sure.

But my journey will involve a subway ride, a walk, a commuter train ride and an Uber. Along the way, I might encounter you. You will know me, for I will be the one intently staring at you and eventually attempting to start a conversation. Please don't be offended, or frightened, for I mean no harm. Indulge me, even for a minute.

You will make me so happy.

REFERENCES

American Cancer Society. 2024. "Key Statistics for Colorectal Cancer." January 29, 2024. https://www.cancer.org/cancer/types/colon-rectal-cancer/about/key-statistics.html#:~:text=Key%20Statistics%20for%20Colorectal%20Cancer,women%20in%20the%20United%20States.

American Society for the Prevention of Cruelty to Animals (ASPCA). 2021. "New ASPCA Survey Shows Overwhelming Majority of Dogs and Cats Acquired During the Pandemic Are Still in Their Homes." May 26, 2021. https://www.aspca.org/about-us/press-releases/new-aspca-survey-shows-overwhelming-majority-dogs-and-cats-acquired-during#:~:text=NEW%20YORK%20–%20The%20ASPCA®,would%20account%20for%20approximately%2023.

AshleyMadison. n.d. Accessed August 7, 2024. https://www.ashleymadison.com.

Bieber, Christy. 2024. "Revealing Divorce Statistics in 2024." *Forbes Advisor,* May 30, 2024. https://www.forbes.com/advisor/legal/divorce/divorce-statistics/.

BrainyMedia Inc. 2024. BrainyQuotes. Accessed August 9, 2024. https://www.brainyquote.com/quotes/george_burns_146499.

BrainyMedia Inc. 2024. BrainyQuotes. Accessed August 7, 2024. https://www.brainyquote.com/quotes/george_carlin_390133.

BrainyMedia Inc. 2024. BrainyQuotes, Accessed August 9, 2024. https://www.brainyquote.com/quotes/george_carlin_386319.

BrainyMedia Inc. 2024. BrainyQuotes. Accessed August 7, 2024. https://www.brainyquote.com/quotes/rodney_dangerfield_154014.

BrainyMedia Inc. 2024. BrainyQuotes. Accessed August 7, 2024. https://www.brainyquote.com/quotes/steven_wright_13804.

Brazer, Joan. 2021. "Comedy Clinic Shows Signs of Life, Needs CPR." *South Florida Sun Sentinel,* updated September 25, 2021. https://www.sun-sentinel.com/1989/02/03/comedy-clinic-shows-signs-of-life-needs-cpr/?clearUserState=true.

Brown, Susan L. 2021. "Bill and Melinda Gates are getting divorced. So are increasing numbers of older Americans." *NBC News,* May 5, 2021. https://www.nbcnews.com/think/opinion/bill-melinda-gates-are-getting-divorced-so-are-increasing-numbers-ncna1266397.

Brown, Tina. 2009. "The Gig Economy." *The Daily Beast,* January 12, 2009. https://www.thedailybeast.com/the-gig-economy.

Buder, Sarah. 2023. "Hygge:": The Danish Concept of Comfort We Need Now More Than Ever." *Afar LLC.* September 28, 2023. https://www.afar.com/magazine/what-is-hygge-everything-to-know-about-denmarks-cozy-lifestyle.

Captain & Tennille. 1975. "Love Will Keep Us Together." Side 1, Track 1on *Love Will Keep Us Together.* A&M Records, LP record.

Carrey, Jim. 2008. "This Much I Know: Jim Carrey." Interview by Tony Horkins. *The Guardian*, October 18, 2008. https://www.theguardian.com/lifeandstyle/2008/oct/19/jim-carrey-interview.

ChatGPT. n.d. Accessed July 2024. https://chatgpt.com/.

City of Foley. n.d. "Welcome to Foley." Accessed August 7, 2024. https://cityoffoley.org/.

Darabont, Frank, director. 1994. *The Shawshank Redemption.* Castle Rock Entertainment. 2 hr., 22 min. https://www.amazon.com/gp/video/detail/amzn1.dv.gti.20b4c3cf-b703-aebb-41bd-0dc683f8c0c8?ref_=imdbref_tt_wbr_ovf__pvt_aiv&tag=imdbtag_tt_wbr_ovf__pvt_aiv-20.

Das, Lina. 2024. "Say Cleese! John Cleese on Buying a Few Extra Years and Re-Opening Fawlty Towers." *Saga*, April 24, 2024. https://www.saga.co.uk/magazine/entertainment/say-cleese-john-cleese-on-buying-a-few-extra-years-and-reopening-fawlty-towers#:~:text=John%20Cleese%20on%20buying%20a%20few%20extra%20years%20and%20re,slow%20down%20the%20ageing%20process.

Dunn, Nic. 2024. "Top 23 TikTok Statistics You Need to Know." *Charle Agency*. May 22, 2024. https://www.charleagency.com/articles/tiktok-statistics/#:~:text=The%20average%20age%20of%20TikTok,16%20to%2024%20years%20old.

Gallup Inc. 2024. "World Happiness Report 2024." *Gallup Inc.* March 20, 2024. https://www.gallup.com/analytics/349487/world-happiness-report.aspx.

Gottlieb, Lori. 2019. *Maybe You Should Talk to Someone: A Therapist, Her Therapist and Our Lives Revealed.* Houghton Mifflin Harcourt.

Handler, Chelsea. 2011. *Lies that Chelsea Handler Told Me.* Grand Central Publishing.

Harrington, Charlie (2018) Conan O'Brien at Dartmouth College (2011) [source code]. https://whatrocks.github.io/commencement-db/2011-conan-o'brien-dartmouth-college/.

Heller, Karen. 2020. "Richard Lewis is Not as Miserable as He Appears. But He's Still Miserable." *The Washington Post*, March 2, 2020. https://www.washingtonpost.com/lifestyle/richard-lewis-interview-curb-your-enthusiasm/2020/02/28/a546dbe0-4de1-11ea-9b5c-eac5b16dafaa_story.html.

Iandoli, Kathy. 2016. "The Rise of 'Mumble Rap': Did Lyricism Take a Hit in 1016?" *Billboard.* December 21, 2016. https://www.billboard.com/music/rb-hip-hop/rise-of-mumble-rap-lyricism-2016-7625631/.

Kim, John. 2021. *Single on Purpose: Redefine Everything. Find Yourself First.* HarperCollins.

Leasaca, Stacey. 2024. "This Small U.S. City was Just Named the Best Place to Retire with No Savings." *Travel & Leisure,* February 22, 2024. https://www.travelandleisure.com/best-places-to-retire-united-states-with-no-savings-study-8597952.

Lizzo. 2022. "It's About Damn Time." Track 2 on *Special.* Nice Life Recording – Atlantic Records, compact disc.

Moore, David. 2003. "Support for NASA Shuttle Flights Remains Firm." *Gallup Inc.* February 17, 2003. https://news.gallup.com/poll/7807/support-nasa-shuttle-flights-remains-firm.aspx.

Neville, Morgan. 2024. *"Steve! (Martin): A Documentary in 2 Pieces."* Season 1, part 2, "Now." Aired March 29, 2024, on Apple TV. https://tv.apple.com/us/show/steve-martin-a-documentary-in-2-pieces/umc.cmc.7kkgskd7j0lomjoqdo97l80ql.

Rogan, Joe, host. 2024. *The Joe Rogan Experience.* #2019 – Abigail Shrier. February 27, 2024. Podcast, 2 hours, 4 min., 44 sec. https://open.spotify.com/episode/5uuOkSoOPd6dCrc52PzVDG.

Roush, Ty. 2024. "Here's Barack Obama's Speech at the DNC In Full." *Forbes.* August 21, 2024. https://www.forbes.com/sites/tylerroush/2024/08/21/heres-barack-obamas-speech-at-the-dnc-in-full/.

Saric, Ivana. 2024. "U.S. hits new low in World Happiness Report." *Axios.* March 19, 2024. https://www.axios.com/2024/03/20/world-happiness-america-low-list-countries.

Schwem, Greg. 2024. "Foley, Alabama, Here Comes Poor Me!" *Eagle Herald,* March 24, 2024. https://www.ehextra.com/opinion/greg-schwem-foley-alabama-here-comes-poor-me/article_17785278-e868-11ee-9c2d-5ff9283f3c44.html.

Scorsese, Martin, director. 2013. *The Wolf of Wall Street.* Paramount Pictures, Universal Pictures. 2013. 2 hr., 14 min. https://www.paramountplus.com/movies/video/Xrg0YkxScIXAetQcKQ023YEWAOuEXtxw/?searchReferral=desktop-web&source=google-organic&ftag=PPM-23-10bfh8c.

Silverman, Sarah. 2010. *The Bedwetter: Stories of Courage, Redemption, and Pee.* HarperCollins.

Syed, Armani. 2023. "Slang Word 'Rizz' is the Oxford University Press Word of the Year." *Time Magazine,* December 4, 2023. https://time.com/6342308/rizz-oxford-university-press-word-of-the-year.

The Rolling Stones. 1969. "You Can't Always Get What You Want." Side 2, Track 4 on *Let It Bleed.* London Records, LP record.

Thriving Center of Psych. 2023. "2024 Mental Health Outlook: Growing Demand for Therapy Among Gen Z & Millennials." December 19, 2023.https://thrivingcenterofpsych.com/blog/gen-z-millennial-therapy-statistics/.

Twain, Mark. 2019. *What Is Man?: And Other Essays*. Omni Publishing.

University of Virginia. 2013. "Valedictory Exercises 2013: Colbert Speech." May 18, 2013. https://majorevents.virginia.edu/finals/archive/stephencolbert2013.

Wallace, David Foster. 1998. *A Supposedly Fun Thing I'll Never Do Again: Essays and Arguments*. Back Bay Books.

Wiking, Meik. 2017. *The Little Book of Hygge*. HarperCollins.

www.ingramcontent.com/pod-product-compliance
Lightning Source LLC
Chambersburg PA
CBHW032044040426
42334CB00039B/1078
9780983025030